Content

1.   VIDEO SURVEILLANCE AND VIDEO ANALYTICS 3

2.   THE UNIFIED INTELLIGENT VIDEO ANALYTICS SUITE 5

3.   STATE OF THE ART 13

4.   APPLICATIONS OF UNIFIED INTELLIGENT VIDEO ANALYTICS SUITE 27

5.   RETURNS ON INVESTMENT 35

6.   THE NEXT GENERATION OF THE UNIFIED INTELLIGENT VIDEO ANALYTICS SUITE 37

7.   VIDEO STREAMING SERVER 44

8.   THE UNIFIED RECORD MANAGEMENT SYSTEM 50

9.   THE PLATFORM 54

10.   THE TECHNOLOGIES 59

11.   VIDEO RECORDING AND STORAGING LEVEL SERVICES 71

12.   VIDEO ANALYTICS PROTOCOL SPECIFICATION FOR EVENT AND METADATA OUTPUT 75

13.   ANALYTICS ALERT SUMMARY AND RULE DEFINITION 94

1. VIDEO SURVEILLANCE AND VIDEO ANALYTICS

The field of electronic surveillance has matured significantly over the past 2 decades, fuelled by the growth of safety and security concerns around the world. Surveillance cameras are being used for a wide variety of applications from national security to securing the home.

Video analytics, also called intelligent video surveillance, is a technology that uses software to automatically identify specific objects, behaviours or attitudes in video footage. It transforms the video into data to be transmitted or archived so that the video surveillance system can act accordingly. It may involve activating a mobile camera in order to obtain more specific data about the scene or simply to send a warning to surveillance personnel so that a decision may be made on the proper intervention required.

As video analytics has dramatically improved its effectiveness as a tool for providing real-time, actionable intelligence in security installations, it's getting serious attention for other uses as well. Its versatility provides excellent return on investment for a wide range of applications, including business intelligence, factory automation, loss prevention, public liability assessments, training, consumer behavior analysis, monitoring traffic flow, and more.

The growing interest in video analytics is fueling new innovations and products, and will continue to do so for some time to come. A report entitled "Global CCTV Market Analysis (2008-2012)" estimates the global CCTV market to exceed US $13 billion in 2009 and the Compounded Annual Growth Rate (CAGR) to be more than 27% during 2009-2012. A report from IMS Research predicts that the video content analysis market will grow to an estimated USD 3.4 billion by 2010. But this is just the tip of the iceberg for the IP video surveillance industry as a whole. According to ABI Research, the video surveillance industry is at a key inflection point between analog and digital technologies and could expand from USD 13.5 billion in revenue in 2006 to USD 46 billion in 2013.1 This means many more businesses and organizations will have the ability to video-enable their operations.

One of the most difficult and expensive aspects of video surveillance has always been the need to have people monitor the cameras. Without someone watching what the cameras are recording, there's no opportunity for immediate intervention or action. After all, what good is recording a shoplifting incident unless someone is observing it and can initiate an apprehension? What good is recording a break-in if you can't mitigate property destruction and theft by responding quickly? Prosecution after the fact is valuable, but not as good as being able to respond to an incident as it is happening.

No matter what the usage, it's getting increasingly difficult and expensive for people to monitor the growing number of video surveillance cameras. Consider all the people you'd need to monitor the 4.1 million surveillance cameras in the United Kingdom – the most watched society on earth. As you might expect, many of these cameras aren't monitored. They just record. And record. And record.

The fact is, as video surveillance systems grow in complexity and scale, they become increasingly demanding in their monitoring requirements. Today advanced compression algorithms, such as H.264, promise to enable even more image data to be transmitted and stored. This makes it easier to have video systems with more channels, but who is going to monitor them? The author believes that by 2012 the volume of video traffic on the Internet will outpace all other traffic from voice and other data. A lot of this will be video surveillance. The million dollar question is who will be doing all the watching?

Even if you could get enough people to do it and afford paying them, chances are, they wouldn't be very effective. Research in the U.S. has shown human observers start showing signs of viewing fatigue after as little as 12 minutes, overlooking up to 45 percent of all activity in the scenes. After 22 minutes, they overlook up to 95 percent.

There's also the issue of all that recorded and stored video. It contains a lot of valuable information for everything from prosecuting crimes to performing market research. But even though video surveillance systems have been around for many years now, extracting useful information is still labor-intensive, time-consuming and tedious. It's an extremely hard task for people to review hours of video surveillance data from dozens (or, in some cases, hundreds) of cameras to find a particular incident that happened in a street, campus or building.

2. THE UNIFIED INTELLIGENT VIDEO ANALYTICS SUITE

Our Unified Intelligent Video Analytics Suite help people to take those challenges of effective video surveillance continue to grow with massive amounts of video being generated (both live and recorded).

- ➢ In a large number of cases recorded video is only watched or reviewed after the event (theft, vandalism, etc) has already occurred.
- ➢ In many instances, manual monitoring of live or recorded video misses key events or suspicious behavior due to operator oversight, error, or fatigue.
- ➢ As cameras get added and the area under surveillance increases, human operators find it a challenge to keep up with the scaled environment.
- ➢ The advent of megapixel cameras makes further demands on the storage and management of recorded video. In the absence of quick decisions, massive amounts of recorded video have to be retained and reviewed, before deletion.

Since our Unified Intelligent Video Analytics Suite do not suffer from human frailties like fatigue and distraction, it can be used to extract meaningful information from video data and alert human operators, thereby giving early warnings of potential risks, even in the case the of unmonitored cameras.

The field of our Unified Intelligent Video Analytics Suite deals primarily with

- ➢ **Extraction of useful information**: Based on certain predefined requirements, the video is analyzed to extract specific information such as events of threat/risk, or events of interest to the user. This information is used in assisting the human operator in making quick and proactive decisions.

- ➢ **Detection of motion/ activity in a video sequence**: By discarding sequences that do not possess relevant activity, redundant information and storage space is greatly reduced. In certain applications, moving objects such as humans or vehicles are tracked over time.

> **Management of the stored data:** Enhanced indexing of stored video frames and richer metadata generation significantly speeds up and improves the search and retrieval of stored video. Video analytics can be used to search and retrieve a particular video sequence in minutes compared to a manual search and retrieval process, which could be significantly longer.

With our unique video analytics technologies and algorithms we patented, our Unified Intelligent Video Analytics Suite, the new generation of video analytic software systems offer sophisticated features including integration with security and information systems. This has led to a large number of new applications in various monitoring environments, which are outside the other similar products.

It supports customizable applications such as

> *Virtual tripwires/intrusion detection* – Alarms are generated when an object violates a virtual tripwire. This is used to secure entrances, perimeters, etc.

> *Motion detection* – Motion detection alerts the operator to potential suspicious activity. Motion detection can also be used to save storage space by discarding video sequences in the absence of relevant activity.

> *Camera tampering* – Cameras that have been intentionally been tampered with (painted, covered, damaged) can be detected when their operation is disrupted, and alarms are generated to notify the operator/user.

> *Shape based object detection and tracking* – Shape based object detection (example – humans, vehicles) are used to detect, label and track the redesignated objects. The labels generated can be used for search and retrieval of recorded video.

> *Theft detection/object removal detection*- When an object under surveillance is removed, an alarm is immediately generated.

> *Loitering detection* – Alerts are generated when humans/objects in a predesignated zone exceed a certain time limit. This can be used to detect

suspicious activity (example - loitering near an ATM machine), trespassing or soliciting.

> *Unattended object detection* – An alarm is generated when an object is detected to be abandoned in a particular area.

> *Traffic/People counter* – This is used to provide traffic statistics or footfall in retail outlets.

> *Density detection* – An alert can be generated if the number of objects/people in a certain area exceeds a certain limit. In the retail environment this tool can be used to gauge the interest in a product. The tool can also be used to open a new retail counter if the number of people in a queue exceeds a certain limit.

> *Illegal parking violation* – Generates an alert if a vehicle is parked in a "No Parking Zone".

> *Stop light violation* – The tool can be used to detect a stop light violation at a traffic light.

> *Lane violation* – If a vehicle enters an unauthorized lane, an alert can be generated.

> *License plate recognition* – The tool can be used to read number/license plates of vehicles for a variety of security or traffic monitoring/enforcement applications.

> *Human face detection* – Once an object has been identified to be a human, the face of the human object can be captured and stored for other applications.

One of the biggest innovations our Unified Intelligent Video Analytics Suite is the increasing success in teaching computers to distinguish among these three events through video analytics and provide real-time alerts: no activity, inconsequential activity, and security issues. It enables video surveillance to do the watching and become a proactive tool that signals the need for immediate intervention by guards, police, or other personnel. It makes video surveillance systems become more efficient when they can recognize situations and trigger alarming and other actions (such as gate and door locking).

With our video analytics acting as a remote observer, patrolling guards can receive notification of an intruder or other event, and potentially act before a crime takes place.

Our Unified Intelligent Video Analytics Suite also turns surveillance video into a gold mine for recording human behavior for use in studying marketing effectiveness, creating training, improving building design, analyzing traffic patterns and many other purposes. Our analytics solutions not only can identify desired incidents, but also can encode video with metadata that makes it fast and easy to search through stored video for the clips that are pertinent to your needs. This can include even behaviors you may not have considered valuable to observe before the video was recorded. Instead of filling up hard drives with "mystery" video no one has the time to view, it can turn surveillance video into a tool that organizations can profit from for everything from research to improving operational efficiency.

One of dramatic improvement in our video analytics is increasing the level of accuracy with which it can perform and the increasing number of tasks they can accomplish for security and business/organizational processes.

The advancements in our Unified Intelligent Video Analytics Suite have increased recognition abilities, dramatically reducing false alerts due to weather, sun positions, and other environment factors. Even better, it can not only distinguish between humans and animals, but between loitering and normal activity. For instance, it can distinguish between someone walking directly from a car and someone hanging around cars – the difference between a customer and a potential thief.

UNIFIED INTELLIGENT VIDEO ANALYTICS SOLUTIONS	
Solution/Product Composition	Our Unified Intelligent Video Analytics Solutions provides capabilities in the following areas: surveillance, recording, analytics, management, archiving, sharing, fixed and mobile access and delivery, image-enabled applications, streaming video, and real-time information – all optimized for wireless broadband networks.
Target Customers	- Security and protection of critical infrastructure like airports, ports, train, bus stations, and water supply infrastructure. - Traffic monitoring/enforcement. - Security at correctional facilities. - Campus security, educational institutions. - Enterprise. - Banking. - Parking monitoring and management. - Construction projects, storage (warehouse), and museums. - Home protection, child monitoring. - Retail

Technology Base	- **Object Detection** in the presence of distraction motion - **2D Object Tracking**: Multi-object tracking with occlusion resolution. - **Object Classification**: View independent object classification. - **3D Object Tracking**: Precise 3D location using standard cameras. - **Multi-scale Tracking**: Automatic PTZ Camera control to track objects. - **Multi-camera Handoff**: The ability to track an object across cameras. - **Face Cataloging**: Captures faces at large distances from the camera. - **XML Metadata Representation** for object and its motion attributes. - **Extensible Engine Architecture** for plug and play video analytics. - **Real Time Event Indexing**: Scene events are instantaneously available for searching in a distributed database environment. - **Web service interfaces for Event Search & Retrieval** support the rapid application development of customer specific applications. - **Scalable Backend System**: unified record management technology allows for both distributed surveillance and scalability.

	Key Features	Description of Feature	Benefit for Customer from Feature
Key Features and Benefits	Mobility and Motion	Send/receive video data while moving, wirelessly	So you can have information when you need it most – to manage an incident scene or event, to make newcomers to a scene/event aware of what they will face
	Collaboration /Sharing	Be able to share what is happening with other responders and central command	So they can see what's going on to help manage response, sometimes without you having to tell them
	Fullness of suite	Our suite of video solutions is more extensive than anyone else's'	So you don't have to have multiple vendors and can use us as your one-stop-shop for mobile video needs
	Modular	Start small, with one or two key components, or implement large-scale solutions immediately	So you can grow your capabilities to serve and protect using video over time, or execute a rapid-deployment as needed.
	High-Quality Video	Optimized for wireless environments and mobility, provides high-resolution images that can be used to obtain stills, and provide reduced start/stops while streaming	So you can possess real-time, actionable video to make more informed decisions, and then use the video and its images as evidence, for future research and analysis, or for training
Solution/Product Marketing Description	Our Unified Intelligent Video Analytics Solutions, the power of pre-emptive intelligence delivered in a comprehensive suite of video solutions that provide extra intelligence such as automatic alerts and video sharing capabilities so you can shift from reactive to proactive decision-making. Attain increased situational awareness for quicker response, better decision-making during an incident, and ultimately, increased safety of responding personnel and the community. Optimized for mobility and motion, Intelligent Video Solutions are sophisticated, robust solutions that will provide mission critical information and improve your daily operations. Intelligent Video Solutions from us deliver an efficient collection and analysis of video data. With this solution, you possess the ability		

	to transform raw video data into actionable, real-time information, share video information seamlessly across multiple networks, all with high-quality video that can provide evidentiary support.

Intelligent Video Solutions is a comprehensive suite of video solutions and applications that includes:

Intelligent Video Surveillance and Control – this next-generation tool for surveillance analysis can monitor multiple video sources and alert personnel when an event has occurred, enabling staff to focus their efforts on investigation and response, rather than watching video monitors. Captured data can be quickly analyzed to give first responders better information. Archived data can be readily available for investigators. Improve response from detection to decision.

Automatic Face Recognition - is solution that captures an image of every people in its view, processes it using a detection and recognition engine, and compares the face against a local violations data base or hot list. If there is a matching image or hit, the software notifies the officer providing details.

Automatic License Plate Recognition - is solution that captures an image of every license plate in its view, processes it using an OCR engine, and compares the plate number against a local violations data base or hot list. If there is a matching number or hit, the software notifies the officer providing details such as make, model and color of the vehicle, along with the type of violation.

Mobile Video Enforcer – Tamper-proof evidence. Video information provided by Mobile Video Enforcer (MVE) gives you evidence for DUI, traffic stops, racial profiling, chases, and other incidents. Be able to prove in court your version of the story. Communities can rest easier knowing that video evidence delivered by MVE proves the integrity of their safety personnel.

Intelligent Traffic Surveillance Solutions – is a sophisticated and robust IP solution that will provide real time mission critical information to improve not only daily operations but also emergency response. Intelligent Traffic Surveillance Solutions delivers efficient collection and analysis of video data. With this solution you will be able to transform raw video data into actionable and real-time information, share data across multiple agencies, and send video data to fixed and mobile users.

Advanced Mobile Video Sharing - this application that helps transform raw video data into actionable, real-time information delivering pre-emptive intelligence and increased situational awareness. Designed for public safety users in motion with one-click sharing capabilities, Atlas provides superior video quality over wireless broadband networks, serving as both an information system and a force multiplier, providing insight to assess situations and increase officer safety. |
| **Value Proposition** | Our Unified Intelligent Video Analytics Solutions is a force multiplier that brings a new level of intelligence by transforming raw video data into actionable, real-time information so you can have increased visibility into your coverage areas, obtain pre-emptive intelligence, and share video while moving. |
| **Key Message** | We brings you a full suite of video solutions that provide real-time, actionable information for more informed decision making, faster. |

Supporting Key Messages	• The power of Pre-emptive Intelligence in sharing actionable, real-time video information • Be everywhere at once with the ability to send and receive streaming video at highway speeds • Anytime, Anywhere Access; Anytime Anywhere Information • Evidentiary-level, high-quality video with the ability to capture still and receive streaming video without starts and stops • Optimized for wireless broadband • Archive video information for later research and analysis, and also for training • Flexible and Scalable with a hybrid approach that allows you to add onto existing systems, or start with an initial small or large system and continue to add as demand for capabilities grows • Easily deployed
Solution/Product Description	Our Unified Intelligent Video Analytics Solutions is a comprehensive suite of solutions that enables the capture, analysis, and storage of video data, delivering pre-emptive intelligence for greater situational awareness, in a mobile environment. Intelligent Video Solutions can serve both an information system and a force multiplier by providing insight needed to assess situations and plan response and monitoring larger areas with existing resources. Optimized for wireless broadband, you can send and receive streaming video at highway speeds, share video, and archive evidentiary quality video information for later research and analysis, and also for training.
Differentiators	**Differentiators** • Over many years of expertise in providing secure systems for mission critical and government customers. We lead the industry in meeting some of the world's most stringent security requirements. • Trusted advisor in Public Safety networking. • Extensive wireless and networking integration expertise. • Customized, Comprehensive solutions with a single point of accountability. • Supported by network design capabilities, specialized processes and tools to assure system reliability required by Mission Critical organizations. • Trusted for decades when lives are on the line. • Backed by an unparalleled support service network that enables users to maximize the utility of the network investment for many years to come. • History of supporting industry standards. We can leverage common platform components to provide the benefits of standardization and interoperability • Provides data solutions tuned to Mission Critical needs of availability, security, and mobility • Innovation

Key Words	Pre-Emptive Intelligence Increased Situational Awareness Video Content Analytics Seamless Mobility Flexible and scalable Modular Rapid deployment Interoperable Complementary Hybrid Pro-active Prevention Mobility	Optimized for wireless Optimized for mobility Real-time information Video sharing Information sharing Comprehensive Force multiplier Intelligence High-Quality Video Evidentiary-quality Mission Critical Wireless Broadband experts

3. STATE OF THE ART

We have witnessed great interest and a wealth of promise in video analytics as an emerging technology. While the last decade laid foundation to such promise, it also paved the way for a large number of new techniques and systems, got many new people involved, and triggered stronger association of weakly related fields. We actually survey almost 300 key theoretical and empirical contributions in the current decade related to video analytics and the spawning of related subfields. We find out significant challenges involved in the adaptation of existing video analytics techniques to build systems that can be useful in the real world. In retrospect of what has been achieved so far, we also conjecture what the future may hold for video analytics research. There are so many areas covered by video analytics. Here, let's focus on image matching & retrieval (object recognition). It is good enough to show that our how good algorithms and technologies are. It is good enough to show that we are the pioneer in video analytics in worldwide.

How difficult is it for people recognize a person from one Billiton of people? In another word, if we give you an image of the person and a book of images for about 1 Billiton persons, how long in average will you take to identify the person from the book? If you are able to look at one image per second from the book, it will take you more than 16 years:

$$1,000,000,000(persons)/60(seconds)/60(minutes)/24(hours)/360(days)/2(average)$$

Even you have 10 times faster, it will still take you more than 1.6 years! How about let computer do the job for you? Then the question will be, giving one image to computer, how soon it can find the identical images from the database which store one Billiton of images.

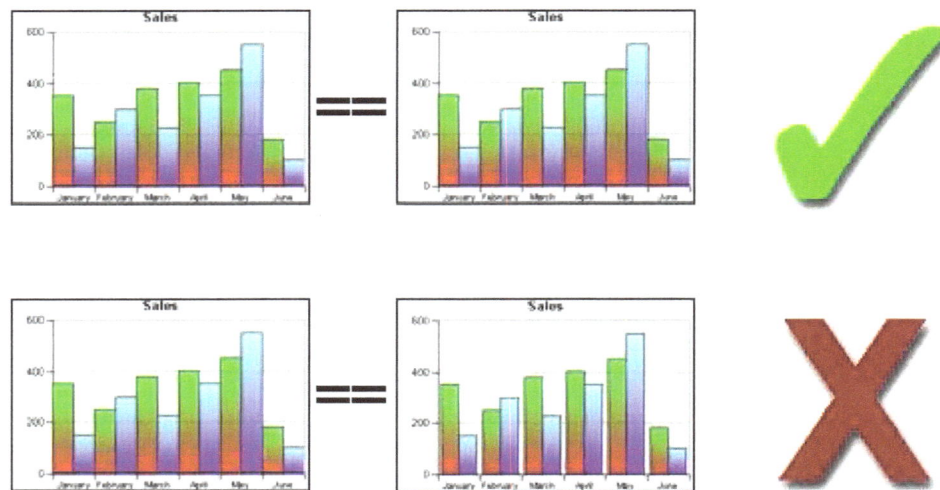

Comparing two images, if at any point, the two pixels did not match then we can safely say that the images are different. If, however, we got to the end of the comparison tests without any mismatches then we can conclude that the two images are indeed identical. This method worked fine but with one major drawback, speed, or rather the lack of it. Comparing two 2000 x 1500 pixel images using this method took over 17 seconds! With over 200 images to compare, this meant that the tests would take nearly an hour to complete. It is much worse than the previous case and we would not be prepared to wait that long – more than 130 years!

How about a faster method to compare the images to allow the tests to complete in a timely manner? Rather than comparing the individual pixels in each image, it would be quicker if we could somehow compare a 'hash' of each image to see if they were identical. As we know, a hash is a unique value of a fixed size representing a large amount of data, in this case the image data. Hashes of two images should match if and only if the corresponding images also match. Small changes to the image result in large unpredictable changes in the hash.

There are many different hashing algorithms. Let's just pick one - the SHA256, which takes a byte array of data as an input parameter and produces a 256 bit hash of that data. By computing and then comparing the hash of each image, we would be quickly able to tell if the images were identical or not. If the images are identical is to compare the two hash values (also stored in byte arrays) to see if they match. Running this new compare method on a 2000 x 1500 pixel bitmap resulted in a comparison time of 0.28 seconds which meant that the automated testing of 200 images now takes only 56 seconds to complete. But it still takes multiple years in our case.

Our motivation to organize things is inherent. Over many years we learned that this is a key to progress without the loss of what we already possess. For centuries, text in different languages has been set to order for efficient retrieval, be it manually in the ancient biblio-theke, or automatically as in the modern digital libraries. But when it comes to organizing pictures, man has traditionally outperformed machines for most tasks. One reason which causes this distinction is that text is man's creation, while typical images are a mere replica of what man has seen since birth, concrete descriptions of which are relatively elusive. Add to this the theory that the human vision system has evolved genetically over many centuries. Naturally, the interpretation of what we see is hard to characterize, and even harder to teach a machine. Yet, over the past decade, ambitious attempts have been made to make computers learn to understand, index, and annotate pictures representing a wide range of concepts, with much progress.

Content-based image retrieval (CBIR), as we see it today, is any technology that in principle helps to organize digital picture archives by their visual content. By this definition, anything ranging from an image similarity function to a robust image annotation engine falls under the purview of CBIR. This characterization of CBIR as a field of study places it at a unique juncture within the scientific community.

CBIR, as a field, has grown tremendously after the year 2000 in terms of the people involved and the papers published. Lateral growth has also occurred in terms of the associated research questions addressed, spanning various fields. Amidst such marriages of fields, it is important to recognize the shortcomings of CBIR as a real-world technology. One problem with all current approaches is the reliance on visual similarity for judging semantic similarity, which may be problematic due to the semantic gap between low-level content and higher-level concepts. Methods for visual similarity, or even semantic similarity (if ever perfected), will remain techniques for building systems. What the average end-user can hope to gain from using such a system is a different question altogether. For some applications, visual similarity may in fact be more critical than semantic. For others, visual similarity may have little significance. Under what scenarios a typical user feels the need for a CBIR system, what the user sets out to achieve with the system, and how she expects the system to aid in this process are some key questions that need to be answered in order to produce a successful system design.

Despite the effort made in the early years of image retrieval research, we do not yet have a universally acceptable algorithmic means of characterizing human vision, more specifically in the context of interpreting images. Hence, it is not surprising to see continued effort in this direction, either building up on prior work or exploring novel directions. Considerations for successful deployment of CBIR in the real world are reflected by the research focus in this area.

By the nature of its task, the CBIR technology boils down to two intrinsic problems: (a) how to mathematically describe an image, and (b) how to assess the similarity between a pair of images based on their abstracted descriptions. The first issue arises because the original representation of an image which is an array of pixel values, corresponds poorly to our visual response, let alone semantic understanding of the image. We refer to the mathematical description of an image, for retrieval purposes, as its signature. From the design perspective, the extraction of signatures and the calculation of image similarity cannot be cleanly separated. The formulation of signatures determines to a large extent the realm for definitions of similarity measures. On the other hand, intuitions are often the early motivating factors for designing similarity measures in a certain way, which in turn puts requirements on the construction of signatures.

In comparison with earlier, pre-2000 work in CBIR, a remarkable difference of recent years has been the increased diversity of image signatures. Advances have been made in both the derivation of new features (e.g., shape) and the construction of signatures based on these features, with the latter type of progress being more pronounced. The richness in the mathematical formulation of signatures grows alongside the invention of new methods for measuring similarity. In the rest of this section, we will first address the extraction of image signatures, and then the methods for computing image similarity based on the signatures. In terms of methodology development, a strong trend which has emerged in recent years is the employment of statistical and machine learning techniques in various aspects of the CBIR technology. Automatic learning, mainly clustering and classification, is used to form either fixed or adaptive signatures, to tune similarity measures, and even to serve as the technical core of certain searching schemes, for example, relevance feedback. We thus not only discuss the influence of learning while addressing fundamental issues of retrieval, but also devote a subsection on clustering and classification in the context of CBIR. Finally, we review different paradigms of searching with emphasis on relevance feedback. An actively pursued direction in image retrieval is to engage humans in the searching process, that is, to include a human in the loop. Although in the very early days of CBIR, several systems were designed with detailed user-preference specifications, the philosophy of engaging users in recent work has evolved toward more interactive and iterative schemes by leveraging learning techniques. As a result, the overhead for a user, in specifying what she is looking for at the beginning of a search, is much reduced.

Today, searchable image data exists with extremely diverse visual and semantic content, spanning geographically disparate locations, and is rapidly growing in size. All these factors have created innumerable possibilities and hence considerations for real-world image search system designers. In recent years, we have put significant effort into understanding the real world implications, applications, and constraints of the technology. Designing an omnipotent real-world image search engine capable of serving all categories of users requires understanding and characterizing user-system interaction and image search, from both user and system points-of-view. We spend continued effort in solving the fundamental open problem of robust image understanding from different fields, such as, computer vision, machine learning, information retrieval, human-computer interaction, database systems, Web and data mining, information theory, statistics, and psychology contributing.

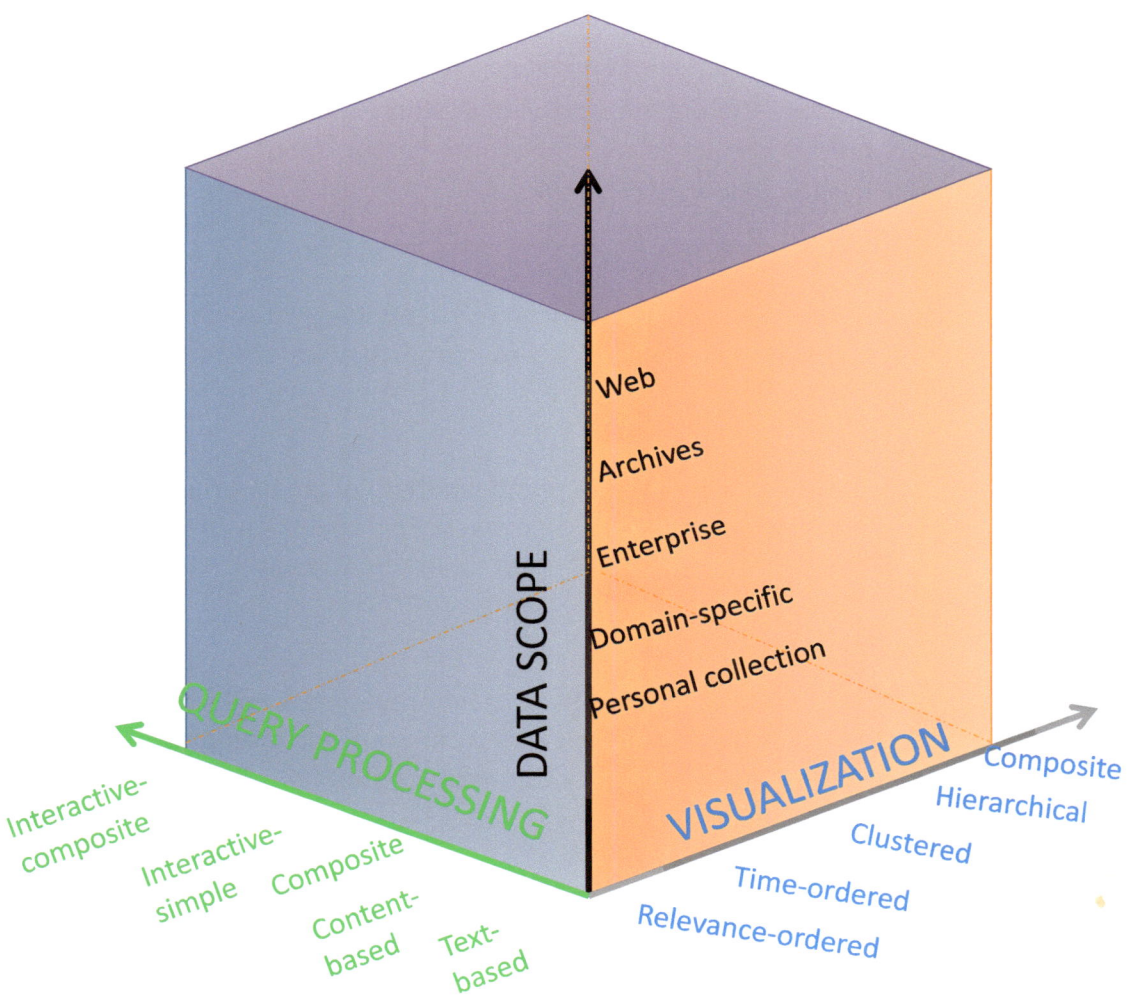

The view of image retrieval from system perspectives

In the proposed user and system spaces, real world image search instances can be considered as isolated points or point clouds, and search sessions can consist of trajectories while search engines can be thought of as surfaces. The intention of drawing cubes versus free 3D Cartesian spaces is to emphasize that the possibilities are indeed bounded by the size of the Web, the nature of user, and ways of user-system interaction. We believe that the proposed characterization will be useful for designing context-dependent search environments for real-world image retrieval systems.

Understanding the nature and scope of image data plays a key role in the complexity of image search system design. Factors such as the diversity of user-base and expected user traffic for a search system also largely influence the design. Along this dimension, we classify search data into the following categories.

- ➢ Personal Collection. This consists of a largely homogeneous collection generally small in size, accessible primarily to its owner, and usually stored on a local storage media.

- ➢ Domain-Specific Collection. This is a homogeneous collection providing access to controlled users with very specific objectives. The collection may be large and hosted on distributed storage, depending upon the domain. Examples of such a collection are biomedical and satellite image databases.

- ➢ Enterprise Collection. We define this as a heterogeneous collection of pictures accessible to users within an organization's intranet. Pictures may be stored in many different locations. Access may be uniform or nonuniform, depending upon the Intranet design.

- ➢ Archives. These are usually of historical interest and contain large volumes of structured or semi-structured homogeneous data pertaining to specific topics. Archives may be accessible to most people on the Internet, with some control of usage. Data is usually stored in multiple disks or large disk arrays.

- ➢ Web. World Wide Web pictures are accessible to practically everyone with an Internet connection. Current WWW image search engines such as Google and Yahoo! images have a key crawler component which regularly updates their local database to reflect on the dynamic nature of the Web. Image collection is semi-structured, non-homogeneous, and massive in volume, and is usually stored in large disk arrays.

In the realm of image retrieval, an important parameter to measure user-system interaction level is the complexity of queries supported by the system. From a user perspective, this translates to the different modalities she can use to query a system. We describe next the various querying modalities, their characteristics, and the system support required thereof.

> Keywords. This is a search in which the user poses a simple query in the form of a word or bigram. This is currently the most popular way to search images, for example, the Google and Yahoo! image search engines.

> Free-Text. This is where the user frames a complex phrase, sentence, question, or story about what she desires from the system.

> Image. Here, the user wishes to search for an image similar to a query image. Using an example image is perhaps the most representative way of querying a CBIR system in the absence of reliable metadata.

> Graphics. This consists of a hand-drawn or computer-generated picture, or graphics could be presented as query.

> Composite. These are methods that involve using one or more of the aforesaid modalities for querying a system. This also covers interactive querying such as in relevance feedback systems.

The aforementioned query modalities require different processing methods and/or support for user interaction. The processing becomes more complex when visual queries and/or user interactions are involved. We next broadly characterize query processing from a system perspective.

> Text-Based. Text-based query processing usually boils down to performing one or

more simple keyword-based searches and then retrieving matching pictures. Processing a free text could involve parsing, processing, and understanding the query as a whole. Some form of natural language processing may also be involved.

> Content-Based. Content-based query processing lies at the heart of all CBIR systems. Processing of query (image or graphics) involves extraction of visual features and/or segmentation and search in the visual feature space for similar images. An appropriate feature representation and a similarity measure to rank pictures, given a query, are essential here.

> Composite. Composite processing may involve both content- and text-based processing in varying proportions.

> Interactive-Simple. User interaction using a single modality needs to be supported by a system. An example is a relevance-feedback-based image retrieval system.

> Interactive-Composite. The user may interact using more than one modality (e.g., text and images). This is perhaps the most advanced form of query processing that is required to be performed by an image retrieval system.

Processing text-based queries involves keyword matching using simple set-theoretic operations, and therefore a response can be generated very quickly. However, in very large systems working with millions of, even billions of pictures and keywords, efficient indexing methods may be required. Indexing of text has been studied in database research for decades now. Efficient indexing is critical to the building and functioning of very large text-based databases and search engines. Research on efficient ways to index images by content has been largely overshadowed by research on efficient visual representation and similarity measures. Most of the methods used for visual indexing are adopted from text-indexing research.

Presentation of search results is perhaps one of the most important factors in the acceptance and popularity of an image retrieval system. We characterize common visualization schemes for image search as follows.

> Relevance-Ordered. The most popular way to present search results is relevanceordered, as adopted by Google and Yahoo! for their image search

engines. Results are ordered by some numeric measure of relevance to the query.

➤ Time-Ordered. In time-ordered image search, pictures are shown in a chronological ordering rather than by relevance. Google's Picasa system for personal collections provides an option to visualize a chronological timeline using pictures.

➤ Clustered. Clustering of images by their metadata or visual content has been an active research topic for several years. Clustering of search results, besides being an intuitive and desirable form of presentation, has also been used to improve retrieval performance.

➤ Hierarchical. If metadata associated with images can be arranged in tree order, it can be a very useful aid in visualization. Hierarchical visualization of search results is desirable for archives, especially for educational purposes.

➤ Composite. Combining consists of mixing two or more of the preceding forms of visualization scheme, and is used especially for personalized systems. Hierarchical clustering and visualization of concept graphs are examples of composite visualizations.

In order to design interfaces for image retrieval systems, it helps to understand factors like how people manage their digital photographs or frame their queries for visual images. User studies on various ways of arranging images for browsing purposes are conducted, and the observation is that both visual-feature-based and concept-based arrangements have their own merits and demerits. Thinking beyond the typical grid-based arrangement of top matching images, spiral and concentric visualization of retrieval results have been explored. For personal images, innovative arrangements of query results based on visual content, time-stamps, and efficient use of screen space add new dimensions to the browsing experience.

Not many image retrieval systems are deployed for public usage, save for Google Image Search or Yahoo! Image Search (which are based primarily on surrounding metadata such as filenames and HTML text). Image analysis and retrieval systems have received widespread public and media interest of late. We believe that the real-world image retrieval lies in exploiting both text- and content-based search technologies. While the former is considered more reliable from a user viewpoint, there is immense potential in combining the two to build robust image search engines that would make the "hidden" part of the Web images accessible.

By the nature of its task, the CBIR (Content Based Image Retrieval) technology boils down to two intrinsic problems: (a) how to mathematically describe an image, and (b) how to assess the similarity between a pair of images based on their abstracted descriptions. The first issue arises because the original representation of an image which is an array of pixel values, corresponds poorly to our visual response, let alone semantic understanding of the image. We refer to the mathematical description of an image, for retrieval purposes, as its signature. From the design perspective, the extraction of signatures and the calculation of image similarity cannot be cleanly separated. The formulation of signatures determines to a large extent the realm for definitions of similarity measures. On the other hand, intuitions are often the early motivating factors for designing similarity measures in a certain way, which in turn puts requirements on the construction of signatures.

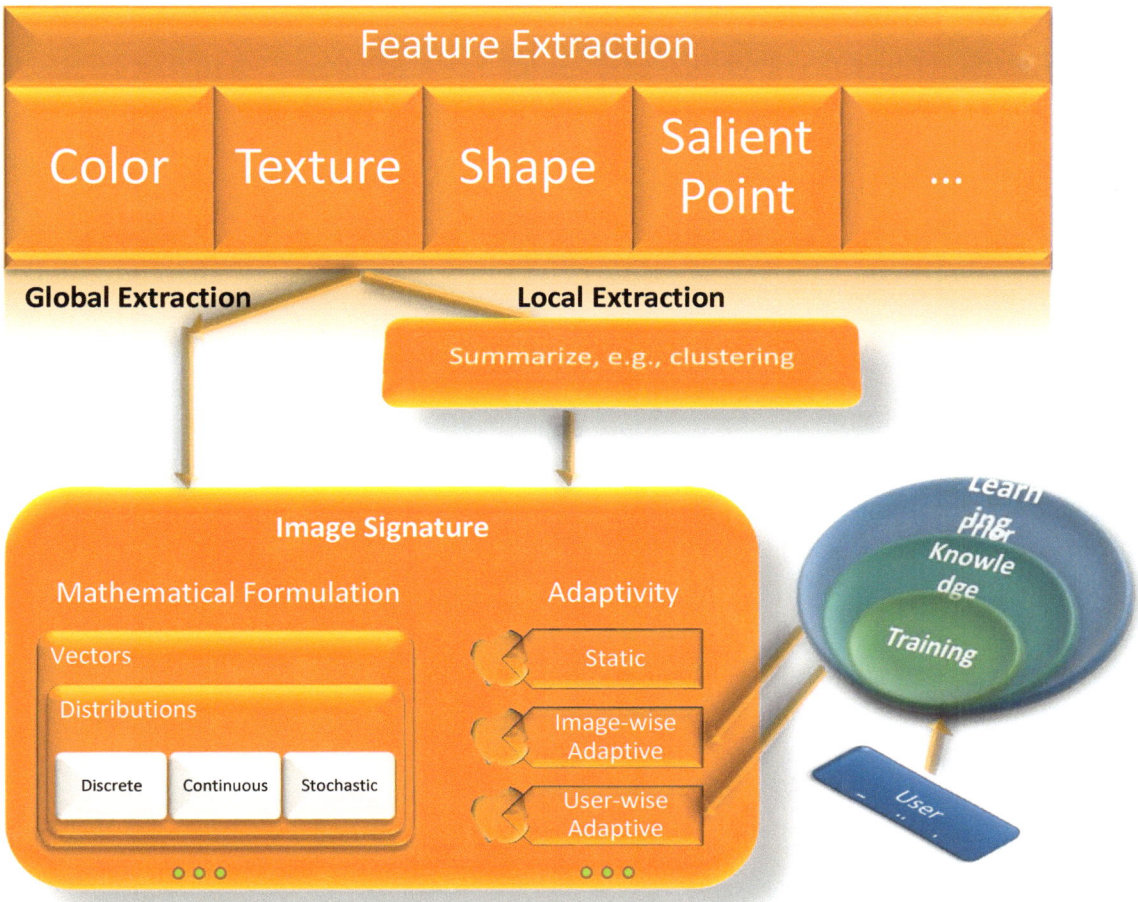

An overview of image signature formulation

In comparison with other algorithms, we have made a remarkable difference in image signatures. Advances have been made in both the derivation of new features (e.g., shape) and the construction of signatures based on these features, with the latter type of progress being more pronounced. We have developed the mathematical formulation of signatures and invented of new methods for measuring similarity. We have addressed the extraction of image signatures, and the methods for computing image similarity based on the signatures. In terms of methodology development, we also employ statistical and machine learning techniques into our models. Automatic learning, mainly clustering and classification, is used to form either fixed or adaptive signatures, to tune similarity measures, and even to serve as the technical core of certain searching schemes, for example, relevance feedback. An actively pursued direction in image retrieval is to engage humans in the searching process, that is, to include a human in the loop. The philosophy of engaging users in our work has evolved toward more interactive and iterative schemes by leveraging learning techniques.

The picture above illustrates the procedure of generating image signatures and the main research problems we have solved. Following the order typical in feature extraction and processing, we present in the following the prominent recent innovations in visual signature extraction.

A feature is defined to capture a certain visual property of an image, either globally for the entire image or locally for a small group of pixels. The most commonly used features include those reflecting color, texture, shape, and salient points in an image, each of which will be discussed shortly. In global extraction, features are computed to capture the overall characteristics of an image. For instance, in a color layout approach, an image is divided into a small number of sub-images and the average color components (e.g., red, green, and blue intensities) are computed for every sub-image. The overall image is thus represented by a vector of color components where a particular dimension of the vector corresponds to a certain sub-image location. The advantage of global extraction is its high speed for both extracting features and computing similarity. However, as evidenced by the rare use of color layout in recent work, global features are often too rigid to represent an image. Specifically, they can be oversensitive to location and hence fail to identify important visual characteristics. To increase the robustness to spatial transformation, the second approach to form signatures is by local extraction and an extra step of feature summarization. In local feature extraction, a set of features are computed for every pixel using its neighborhood (e.g., average color values across a small block centered around the pixel). To reduce computation, an image may be divided into small, non-overlapping blocks, and features are computed individually for every block. The features are still local because of the small block size, but the amount of computation is only a fraction of that for obtaining features around every pixel.

Color features with emphasis on exploiting color spaces (e.g., LUV) that seem to coincide better with human vision than the basic RGB color space. Color features have focused more on the summarization of colors in an image, that is, the construction of signatures out of colors. A set of color and texture descriptors tested for inclusion in the MPEG-7 standard, and well suited to natural images and video. These include histogram-based descriptors, spatial color descriptors, and texture descriptors suited for retrieval.

Texture features are intended to capture the granularity and repetitive patterns of surfaces within in a picture. For instance, grassland, brickwalls, teddy bears, and flower petals differ in texture, by smoothness as well as patterns. Their role in domain-specific image retrieval, such as in aerial imagery and medical imaging, is particularly vital due to their close relation to the underlying semantics in these cases.

Shape is a key attribute of segmented image regions, and its efficient and robust representation plays an important role in retrieval. Synonymous with shape representation is the way in which such representations are matched with each other.

Closely associated with these methods are approaches that model spatial relations among local image entities for retrieval. Features based on local invariants such as corner points or interest points, traditionally used for stereo matching, are being used in image retrieval as well.

According to mathematical formulations, we summarize the types of signature roughly into vectors and distributions. Histograms and region-based signatures can both be regarded as sets of weighted vectors, and when the weights sum up to one, these sets are equivalent to discrete distributions (i.e., discrete in the sense that the support is finite). We focus on region-based signature and its mathematical connection with histograms because it is the most exploited type of image signature.

It is quite intuitive that the same set of visual features may not work equally well to characterize, say, computer graphics and photographs. To address this issue, learning methods have been used to tune signatures either based on images alone or by learning on-the-fly from user feedback. We categorize image signatures according to their adaptivity into static, image-wise adaptive, and user-wise adaptive. Static signatures are generated in a uniform manner for all the images. Image-wise adaptive signatures vary according to the classification of images. Specifically, images are classified into several types first, and then signatures are formed from different features for these types.

Over the years, we find out that it is too ambitious to expect a single similarity measure to produce robust, perceptually meaningful ranking of images. As an alternative, we attempt to augment the effort with learning-based techniques. Image classification or categorization has often been treated as a preprocessing step for speeding-up image retrieval in large databases and improving accuracy, or for performing automatic image annotation. Similarly, in the absence of labeled data, unsupervised clustering has often been found useful for retrieval speedup as well as improved result visualization. While image clustering inherently depends on a similarity measure, image categorization has been performed by varied methods that neither require nor make use of similarity metrics. Image categorization is often followed by a step of similarity measurement, restricted to those images in a large database that belong to the same visual class as predicted for the query. In such cases, the retrieval process is intertwined, whereby categorization and similarity matching steps together form the retrieval process. Similar arguments hold for clustering as well, due to which, in many cases, it is also a fundamental "early" step in image retrieval.

With our algorithms in proper configuration, we are actually able to achieve the amazing performance, which is we can retrieve the same and top xx (for example top 10, top 20) most similar images from millions, even billions of images within seconds. Sometime, it is even less than 1 second. Media relevant to the broad area of multimedia retrieval and annotation includes, but is not limited to, images, text, free text (unstructured, e.g., paragraphs), graphics, video, and any conceivable combination of them. Thus far, we have encountered a multitude of techniques for modeling and retrieving images, and text associated with these images. Precious little multimodal fusion has been attempted in the context of image retrieval and annotation. This opens avenues for exploring novel user interfaces, querying models, and resulting visualization techniques pertinent to image retrieval, in combination with other media. Having said that, our multimodal fusion has indeed been attempted in more obvious problem settings within video retrieval.

4. APPLICATIONS OF UNIFIED INTELLIGENT VIDEO ANALYTICS SUITE

Our intelligent video surveillance systems use mathematical algorithms to detect moving objects in an image and filter non-relevant movements. With that, we can create a database that records the attributes of all the objects detected and their movement properties. Decisions are made by the system or events of interest are searched in archived footage based on rules (e.g., if a person oversteps a boundary, send an alert).

Today, video surveillance networks have a greater number of cameras. For large infrastructures, such as a mass transit system, over a thousand surveillance cameras may be deployed. These installations represent a huge amount of video to transmit, view and archive, making it impossible for a human monitor to analyze all of these video recordings in order to detect suspicious behaviour or events. This is especially true since security control centre personnel are also required to manage other tasks, such as access control, issuance of badges/keys/permits, handling emergency calls, following up on fire alarms, radio communications control, etc.

Several studies show the limits of human surveillance. After only 20 minutes of looking at and analyzing video surveillance screens, the attention of most people falls below an acceptable level. A monitor cannot attentively follow 9 to 12 cameras for over 15 minutes. Certain studies report that the ratio between the number of screens and the number of cameras can be between 1:4 and 1:78 in certain video surveillance networks11. The probability of reacting immediately to an event captured by a surveillance camera network is estimated at 1 out of 1,000. That is why, historically, video surveillance is mainly a post-event investigation tool.

In our suite, it has many advantages:

 ➢ It operates 24/7.
 ➢ It can trigger an alarm that will be handled by a human operator or order the movement or zooming in of a camera for a more accurate surveillance of the event, thereby providing real time instead of post-event intervention.
 ➢ It reduces the bandwidth and archiving space needed by transmitting or recording

only data on relevant events.

➢ It relieves security personnel from continuous surveillance.
➢ It enables a quick search of relevant events in the archived video footage.
➢ It makes it possible to identify objects in a scene and follow their activity (situation awareness).

Sectors of Application

Today, surveillance cameras can be found in different public and private places, such as apartment buildings, shops, parking lots, railroad/bus stations, airports, roads, mass transit, banks, etc. Casinos appear as pioneers in the deployment of large video surveillance systems. Our video surveillance can be used by public services (police, transportation, administration). It can be also adopted by companies looking to protect strategic assets, such as refineries, nuclear power plants, dams, agrifood plants and pharmaceutical complexes.

Many other surveillance systems are deployed on small scale. This type of system can be found at the corner store, in small shops or in a private home. For monitoring minor crimes (e.g., assaults, vandalism, theft), video surveillance is used primarily for post-incident investigation. This level of surveillance requires simple, often analogue technologies that do not involve video intelligence.

Our unified intelligent video analytics suite is designed to be deployed in middle scales to very large scales.

Monitoring of apartment buildings or larger shops often requires a more extensive camera system. The goal of surveillance is mainly to monitor access paths, parking lots, and in the case of stores, departments and points of sale. Video surveillance is used in these locations mainly for investigation purposes. However, these users would like to obtain surveillance systems able to generate alerts in real time for immediate intervention. Our video analytics system is therefore a breakthrough in these sectors. For this clientele, return on investment is a determining factor in buying intelligent video surveillance equipment.

Large-scale video surveillance is found in cities and neighbourhoods, transportation systems, university campuses, at major events (festivals, economic summits, Olympic games, etc.), with extensive security parameters. It requires dozens, even hundreds of cameras to be deployed. These cameras must sometimes be accessible to hundreds of security responders from different government agencies, police forces or emergency services. In these facilities, video surveillance is in addition to a plethora security and monitoring systems: access control, fires, telephony, radio communications, geomatic systems, etc. Given the number of video cameras involved and the scale of the emergency interventions, our video analytics system can be particularly conducive to be used in these applications for the automated processing of video flow generating alarms when suspicious events are noticed. Because adding our analytical software is more easily foreseeable there and the return on investment of our surveillance system in these infrastructures are often vast.

Our video surveillance system can be used in mobile units, such as patrol cars, ambulances, buses, etc. with wireless video signal transmission to a security control centre.

❖ **Government and Public Security**

The different levels of government must ensure the safety of the population and of public infrastructures. On the national level, it will be used, for example, to monitor the following:

➢ Sensitive infrastructures
➢ Borders
➢ Government buildings and sites
➢ Laboratories
➢ Military bases
➢ Prisons

Locally, video surveillance is set up in several cities around the world to monitor crimes and for use as an emergency intervention tool. It also helps to ensure security during large gatherings (shows, demonstrations, sporting events, etc.). London is the city the most often cited for the number of cameras deployed in its streets. Video surveillance is also used to manage parking, especially to monitor parking permits, the application of rules, the detection of theft, vandalism or misdemeanours, and to control access.

Video surveillance is widely used by controlling forces to conduct investigations, monitor people and vehicles sought, and detect dangerous or criminal activities. It can also be found on board patrol cars to verify police interventions.

Cameras can be increasingly found along stretches of road to monitor traffic and detect incidents, dangerous behaviour or violations. Montréal has a multi-camera system and vehicle detection stations to follow traffic conditions in real time and automatically detect incidents13.

Our intelligent video surveillance can fully support many sectors of the government for: identifying individuals and vehicles, counting people and monitoring crowds, recognizing suspicious or violent behaviour (fights, misdemeanours), detecting intrusions, and monitoring roads. More advanced analyses, such as computer recognition of emotions or if an individual is telling a lie, are also anticipated.

❖ Education

Video surveillance is increasingly found in academic institutions. It is used to oversee the safety of teachers and students, as well as to protect assets from vandalism and theft. Tragic school killings, such as at Columbine, in the US, and here in Quebec at Polytechnique and Collège Dawson, have highlighted the importance of monitoring school campuses more closely. These campuses may be extensive, especially in the case of universities, and be comprised of several buildings, accesses and parking lots to monitor. In this environment, video surveillance is used in particular to:

- ➢ monitor access to the institution's perimeter, which may be extensive, such as in the case of a university campus;
- ➢ monitor equipment and data;
- ➢ detect and follow acts of vandalism, theft, misdemeanours and inappropriate behaviour;
- ➢ recognize license plates;
- ➢ support criminal investigations;
- ➢ control access.

Since educational institutions often have an IP network infrastructure, it will be beneficial for them to set up our intelligent video surveillance systems.

❖ **Retail Trade**

Retail trade is a growing market for video surveillance, which is used for both internal (store, warehouse) and external (parking lot) security. Even the smallest shops have cameras to at least keep video evidence in case of theft or an incident. In chain stores, much more sophisticated video surveillance systems are set up for centralized monitoring of different locations. For the entire sector, video surveillance is aimed primarily at:

- ➢ monitoring registers and transactions (employee theft and fraud);
- ➢ protecting material goods and infrastructures;
- ➢ monitoring inventory and wares (deliveries);
- ➢ protecting staff and clients;
- ➢ controlling access to locked areas;
- ➢ checking emergency situations (fire, alarms, etc.);
- ➢ monitoring parking lots, vehicles, entries and exits.

Given the high risk of theft and attacks to which retailers are exposed, as well as the resulting significant losses, video surveillance becomes an essential tool for ensuring the security of employees and merchandise. This market also presents a real potential for our video analytics system. For example, there are systems that combine video information and data from the register to check that the items taken out by clients have indeed been invoiced. This technology also makes it possible to prevent fraud involving cashiers at points of sale.

Our intelligent video surveillance is also increasingly used for non-security purposes, such as managing operations and market launch. In this context, our video analytics system is used in particular to count clients, analyze their behaviour and in-store movements, and compile statistics on consumer habits.

❖ **Transportation**

The security and smooth operation of airports, railroad/bus stations, ports and mass transit systems are critical for a country's economy. A security incident can seriously upset operations and result in significant losses. Given the large flows of passengers that use transportation systems and the extent of their infrastructures, these systems face extraordinary security challenges. Terrorist acts committed in different transportation systems around the world have exacerbated these challenges.

Our intelligent video surveillance system targets the transportation sector by offering different adapted functions: detecting an intrusion in a controlled perimeter or area, detecting people entering an exit ramp, detecting abandoned luggage, recognizing faces, counting people, recognizing license plates for monitoring access to parking lots, detecting suspicious behaviour (loitering, vandalism, graffiti), detecting people in lanes.

❖ **Airports**

Following the events of September 11, 2001, security measures were tightened, especially at large airports, and new technologies were deployed. For airports, the priority consists in controlling access to secure areas, in particular access to airplanes, and also in ensuring the safety of passengers, personnel and the property within the perimeter (runways, parking lots, access routes, etc.)

For example, our video surveillance system can be used above all to assist with emergency interventions. When an incident is reported, a mobile camera pivots to follow the operations live from a security control centre. Access control is provided primarily by biometric identification technologies (fingerprints, iris recognition), and the use of smart cards. Videos and video events can be archived and also can be used as evidence in police force investigations. Our intelligent functions can be in place consist of counting people to assess, for example, processing times at customs, as well as for license plate recognition in order to take stock of vehicles in parking lots and to detect theft.

❖ **Stations and Public Transportation**

The deployment of our video surveillance system in railroad/bus stations and public transportation is mainly to monitor access routes, platforms, rails and tunnels, parking lots and all auxiliary service structures. It is connected to other access monitoring systems and security devices to oversee the protection of passengers, personnel and infrastructures. The video can be viewed live from the security control centre, or at a later time for investigations following security incidents. Our video analytics system can be used for automated detection of people on the tracks and states, detecting suspicious packages, monitoring doors and recognizing suspicious behaviour.

❖ **Ports**

As for other transportation systems, in ports, our intelligent video surveillance can be used to protect passengers and personnel, to monitor comings and goings in the perimeter and to identify vehicles in this perimeter.

❖ **Bank Setting**

Our intelligent video analytics surveillance system can be widely used for bank security. The presence of our system first acts as a deterrent to committing armed robbery and assault. Should a crime occur, archived video footage is used to investigate and identify the perpetrators. Automated bank machines are prime targets for criminal acts. Our system helps to detect fraud, such as, for example, the installation of a device to read the magnetic information on bank cards.

In a bank setting, our intelligent video surveillance can increase monitoring effectiveness. It provides for monitoring of all branches in order to detect suspicious individuals or behaviour. It also makes it possible to find, among other things, all video footage from all branches where a certain individual appears using face recognition techniques.

❖ **Gaming Industry and Casinos**

Casinos and gaming centres will benefit greatly when they use our intelligent video surveillance system to protect clients and premises, as well as to detect cheating, heists, cash register theft and other crimes resulting in losses. It can also been used as evidence to assess the validity of actions for damages against the gaming institution.

Since casino monitoring requires watching the behaviour of many people in a crowded environment, our intelligent video surveillance system is an dramatically interesting way of helping security personnel do their job. Face and gesture detection and recognition are part of the useful analytical functionalities for this environment.

❖ **Other**

Our video surveillance system can used in many other environments, such as in stores and to monitor buildings. It is most often used to film access routes and parking lots, monitor material valuables and ensure employee and client protection.

It can also be used in healthcare to help with interventions. It can even be found in ambulances and used in combination with other measuring instruments to monitor a patient remotely. Our analytical solution can detect the movement of helicopters landing on the site of an American hospital.

5.   RETURNS ON INVESTMENT

Video analytics provides excellent return on investment (ROI). Waste Management, a U.S. recycling and waste management company with 2,200 locations, calculates their video analytics system saved them $7.5 million in 2007. The system enabled them to reduce staff, travel and equipment, plus achieve faster response to incidents.

But that's only part of the picture. Video analytics also enables repurposing video for business intelligence. The same company (Waste Management) reports its accounting and operations departments use video analytics for business optimization activities such as monitoring point-of-sale displays and improving traffic patterns.

Retailers are a large market for video analytics. They use it to obtain information about customer flow, hot spots (places within the store that are most frequented by customers), line lengths, product placement, and in-store advertising effectiveness. Video analytics has advanced enough to actually identify customer "eyeball connections" with merchandise.

Other typical uses of video analytics include:

> Companies in the U.S., such as Brickstream and Shoppertrak, install video analytics systems to collect information about customer behavior in banks, retail stores, grocery stores, gasoline stations, and other locations.
> The Smithsonian Museum uses a new camera system with video analytics to track traffic patterns and devise ways to increase museum store visits.
> Advertising agencies use video analytics to measure the impact of an ad to a passerby or bystander. These solutions can detect a face (including if it's male or female) as well as the face's movement – whether it's looking at the ad on the wall, and if so, for how long.
> Toll roads employ video analytics to study vehicle flow and respond to traffic incidents.
> Chicago METRA Electric District (METRA) in Chicago, Illinois (one of North America's largest city transit companies) is installing high resolution cameras and video analytics to continuously inspect METRA's train pantographs (the metal frame on top of an electric locomotive that picks up electricity from cables hanging above the track). The video analytics detects suspicious anomalies suggesting

defects.

There are hundreds more examples. One important key to success and good ROI in implementing video analytics is finding a solution provider who can understand your needs and effectively integrate analytics into your operations. This is a relatively new field and it's important for vendor and customer to work closely together to achieve the best results.

6. THE NEXT GENERATION OF THE UNIFIED INTELLIGENT VIDEO ANALYTICS SUITE

The field of video analytics is expanding rapidly, and there are several applications that can be enabled in the future. We are already working on the next generation of our Unified Intelligent Video Analytics Suite to take several challenge areas including news video, meetings, surveillance video, and aerial video. The goal was to create a semantic, searchable info-base from video, exploiting multimodal information such as text and speech. We also working on enabling additional applications based on our solution to address some open problems that are described in the following sections.

Moving Cameras

Current embedded analytics are mostly computed on static scenes with fixed cameras, and are based on the concept of background subtraction. Moving cameras that are either hand-held or vehicle-mounted must separate camera motion from object motion. We have been doing various patented techniques to estimation of camera motion. These techniques are computationally intensive and may require working memory that has been beyond the scope of most commercially viable embedded processors. With the advance vision processor, and the advances in automotive vision and aerial surveillance, those algorithms can work on real-time mosaicing or frame-to-frame camera motion computation on a single video channel.

Vehicle-mounted cameras for surveillance and operational purposes are common in law enforcement and public transit. These views exhibit significant parallax, and affine transformation models cannot be used to estimate frame-to-frame motion accurately. Feature tracking and homography computations have been shown to work in these cases although they are still limited in the range of camera motion and the duration for which accurate tracking may be done. Accurate tracking over several minutes and hours from a vehicle or aircraft-mounted camera remains an open problem. This challenge is further compounded by the limitations of embedded systems.

With the easy availability of low-cost CMOS imagers, our research shows that stereo vision systems can be developed that can mitigate several issues with cameras mounted on moving vehicles. Our algorithms can be used in the embedded stereoscopic vision system that performs background modeling and stereo correlation from a pair of imagers in real-time. This can reduce issues with clutter and occlusion, and can aid in segmentation by incorporating depth information.

Multi-Camera Tracking

Applications in surveillance, retail, and transportation can benefit from track association across views and cameras. For instance, for surveillance it may be important to track the motion of people and vehicles over a large region that has multiple cameras. Retail environments tend to have multiple nonoverlapping cameras. In order to track customer activities and behavior, our research project correlate the same customer across multiple views, and conduct an online discriminative model to be constructed for re-acquisition and association of the person between views.

The new project will work with the active tracking systems employ pan-tilt-zoom (PTZ) cameras that can simultaneously detect and track objects, while controlling the motion of the camera to keep a subject centered in the view. It takes the challenges by occlusion and clutter as well. Camera motion will be factored out while the pan-tilt unit is in motion. Scale ambiguities from zooming can cause difficulty with target tracking. For busy scenes with multiple targets, the tracker may occasionally jump between targets, causing erratic motion of the pan-tilt head, or track switching.

Multi-camera tracking may be done with overlapping cameras or nonoverlapping cameras. In the case of overlapping cameras, we handle the tracked object to be correlated across different views. Each view may see a different portion of the target. Camera calibration can aid with such tracking. Calibration-free association of objects across overlapping but widely differing viewpoints remains challenging. This is further complicated if the scene has multiple objects that may be occluding or passing one another.

Multi-camera tracking across nonoverlapping cameras, we conduct the construction of a fingerprint or signature for each object that is being tracked. So we may have the flexibility of providing similar views of the object; therefore, similar features would be visible from each camera. However, finding discriminative features among objects of a single class is challenging. Our new patented technique to track vehicles from roughly overhead nonoverlapping views and show good results over a set of 200 vehicles captured at different times of the day.

Multi-camera tracking and association over nonoverlapping, uncalibrated cameras with different viewpoints remains an active research for us. An additional challenge occurs if multiple classes of objects, such as persons and vehicles need to be tracked simultaneously.

Scene Understanding

Current applications of video analytics build upon computer vision and pattern recognition technologies, and are able to "perceive" changes and interpret them to report discrete events. This is primarily based on the analysis of foreground pixels and their motion. We are working on using background pixels to provide context that can be exploited to gain a semantic understanding of the scene.

Our next generation video analytics system observes the scene, and classifies and tracks people and vehicles, and it can infer the 3D characteristics of background objects. Scene geometry estimation can be done with uncalibrated cameras, if certain simplifying assumptions can be made such as the presence of a ground plane where pedestrians and vehicles are detected. Further, output from tracking can indicate background objects that cause occlusions. Such front-back relationships between background objects can provide cues for depth estimation.

We use a statistical framework that simultaneously infers object identity, surface orientation and camera viewpoint using a single uncalibrated image. A key challenge for such approaches is reliable segmentation and localization of foreground objects. Additionally, a scene model that is representative of the content in the scene must be constructed online. Robust online scene modeling and maintenance over long periods of time continues to be a challenge.

Our future research based on scene understanding will be able to address the problem of converting video to text. A narrative of a video sequence provided in natural language would mimic a human observer. It is conceivable that such a system could surpass human abilities in specific scenarios.

Search and Retrieval

The combination of inexpensive video cameras, efficient compression technology and affordable storage solutions has resulted in increasingly larger amounts of video data being stored and archived. In surveillance, it is common to find hundreds of video streams being stored for weeks or months.

With video driving a large portion of growth in Internet traffic and usage, our analytics system will organize, analyze, interpret, index and retrieve video. We use high-level semantic queries for video that is used to retrieve video segments from an enormous corpus of video content with highly relevant results. The user experience would be similar to text searching on the web today. The volume of video content generated will far exceed the capability of offline algorithms to analyze it. Therefore, our online video analytics patented algorithms compute rich metadata using streaming video.

Our techniques for video indexing and retrieval depend on the computation of features such as color histograms, texture, shape, and geometry. Query-by-content and query-by-example systems require a user to submit an exemplary image, the result of which is a set of similar images. Natural language queries will be supported. Further, our system addresses image retrieval, and exploits the temporal nature of video. Video queries that describe entire activities such as "find me all people that climb on a bus and have a blue backpack" require semantic analysis of the scene, and feature descriptors that span multiple frames of a video sequence.

Next Generation Video Analytics Algorithms Improvements

Given the explosion in the amount of video footage captured by security, the need to develop automatic methods for detecting suspicious people, objects or events so that only sequences relevant for human analysis are submitted has been widely noted. Existing techniques are promising, but few of them are currently commercially used in real case scenarios.

With respect to our research, our patented algorithms to video surveillance are not only partial solutions dealing with part of the video surveillance problem, but also operate under near-reality conditions. In the next generation video analytics system, we are working our system works well in video analytics is movement detection, the detection of specific objects, license plate recognition done from specialized systems, and the detection of certain specific behaviours (walking, running, carrying an object).

The following will be developed and improved:

➢ Near-real-time detection and recognition, i.e., in the minutes following the incident (especially important for the security of sensitive infrastructures or during major events).
➢ More specifically, real-time face recognition (25 to 30 frames/sec).
➢ Face recognition in a crowd. This requires an image with sufficient resolution that can be accessible with the megapixel cameras now available on the market.
➢ People counting in crowded environments and under various angles-of-view.
➢ Tracking of specific objects in crowded scenes (an individual in a crowd or a vehicle in traffic).
➢ Tracking of hinged bodies for understanding activities.
➢ Recognition of more complex behaviours, relevant for security purposes.
➢ Segmentation of areas of colour. For example, colour information on a car may improve the performance of the plate recognition algorithm. It may also be used to recognize different pieces of an individual's clothing.
➢ For detection and recognition, the fusion of different video data (e.g., combining face recognition with gait recognition), or the merger of video data with those obtained by different systems (temperature sensors, biometric systems, etc.), are the methods being built on.

Our video analytics algorithms function only for fixed cameras, good resolution and with adequate and constant lighting, but will consider these situations, such as sudden camera changes (spider webs, dust, moved camera). The robustness and accuracy of most of the existing detection, tracking and recognition algorithms are vital when dealing with changing environmental conditions. In order to be adopted by consumers, our intelligent video surveillance systems will be strong enough to deal with different weather conditions, adjust to lighting changes (natural and artificial) of the scene and adapt to hardware and software failures.

Vision for an Analytics-Powered Future

Over the next decade, we expect that video analytics will go mainstream and will be a part of our daily lives. Video sensors will be ubiquitous, embedded in everything including buildings, appliances, automobiles, furniture and possibly clothing. Embedded analytics and communication stacks in these sensors will enable them to collaborate to achieve specific tasks autonomously. The intelligence embedded in these networks of sensors will allow them to be tasked to "watch" and "react" autonomously. Intelligent traffic systems will achieve flow control by adaptively routing traffic around hotspots. Analytics-driven sensors embedded in automobiles will automatically interpret traffic signs, and alert the driver to speed limits, or possibly regulate speed. Analytics sensors embedded in clothing will be context aware, and will alert a person to activities occurring outside the human field-of-view; the equivalent of having unblinking eyes behind your head!

The human-machine interface that enables natural interaction with these capabilities will be critical to the adoption and use of analytics. The best interfaces are those that are transparent and enable users to focus on the task, rather than on learning the interface. Widespread usage will dictate that analytics not be obtrusive; rather, it would be best for end users to not realize the presence of machine intelligence. For social acceptance, it will be critical to address privacy issues with video. Embedded analytics in which the sensors interpret video at its source, and only forward key metadata instead of images, will mitigate concerns about privacy.

Applications of video analytics will extend beyond current markets in surveillance, retail, and transportation. Most consumer video today consists of broadcast, film and sports content which has a very wide variety of scene characteristics and subject motion. We imagine a future where a user will be able to pose a high level query to retrieve a specific moment in a game, or search for a specific type of scene in a film either through natural language or by presenting examples of similar scenes. These applications will run on increasingly faster embedded processors, which will be capable of running for extended periods using very low power, and will be able to communicate with their surroundings.

7. VIDEO STREAMING SERVER

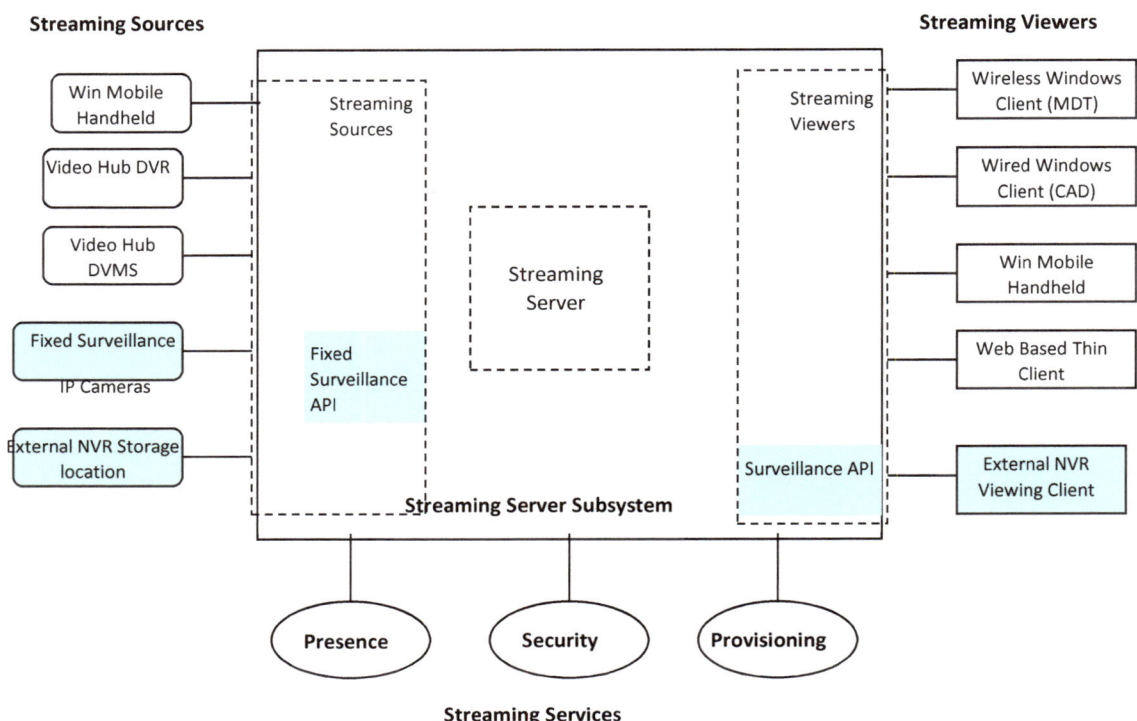

Video Streaming Server provides the business and market features for Video Streaming Services for the Video Hub and our Products:

- Provides Video Streaming Services for desktop, handheld and back office clients.

- Includes a Video Surveillance API for interfacing Video Hub, video applications with external fixed Video Surveillance platforms.

- Provides Video Streaming functionality for Video Hub, video applications, and handheld platforms.

- Provides Video Presence functionality for Video Hub, video applications, and handheld platforms.

- Provides User Authentication and Access Authorization for PremierOne CAD/Mobile, MCCP applications, and other handheld platforms.

Streaming Platforms

- Streaming Server can be co-resident on a Video Hub DVMS or other Server Platform

- Streaming source/viewer can run on a Windows XP/7 based Client with other applications such as Video Hub, CAD, Records applications.

- Streaming source/viewer can be resident on a win mobile handheld device along with other applications.

- A limited functionality Viewer (view only with limited presence) shall be available via a web based client for access to streaming sources.

- The Streaming Service shall scale to concurrently support the following

    o 500 Video Hub DVRs (source and viewing functionality)

    o 100 handheld devices

    o 50 wired viewers (Video Hub Back Office, Dispatch, etc.)

    o 50 wireless viewers (thin clients, MDT only viewing clients, etc.)

- Streaming Service shall be designed to take advantage of source multicast where supported (e.g. LTE)

- Wireless clients shall be 3G/4G WAN capable.

Streaming Live/Recorded Video

- Viewing live sources (with access to pre-buffer of the current recording) with a directory of available sources.

- Requesting a recorded video to be streamed from a remote storage location (Video Hub DVR, Video Hub DVMS, NVR storage location via API) with access to basic search/query functionality to locate video.

- Architecturally having the DVR as the Streaming Source is preferred which will require the DVR to be WAN enabled.

- Provide the streaming source with an indication that it is streaming video

- Provide the streaming source with information on what viewers are streaming its video

- All streaming sources will stream synched video and audio for live and recorded video streams

- The Video Streaming Service will support the streaming of fixed and dynamic metadata along with the video/audio

- Streaming service should support seamless switching between mobile VPNs

Video Quality

- Live video needs to have low delay, < 500ms (errors/degradation is acceptable)

- Recorded video can have moderate delay, < 5sec (which should allow for support for higher quality of video stream vs. live)

- Support for remote viewer to control the frame rate and spatial quality of streamed video.

- Support for rate adaptation upon session set up (static), or auto/dynamic based on network signal strength.

Session Initiation & Media Distribution

- User pushes live/recorded video to a viewer

- User pulls live/recorded video from a source

- User pushes to a remote user(s) a message with a link to a video stream

- User pushes video to a group of users (not necessarily a conference set-up)

- System supports the establishment of pre-defined viewing groups

Simultaneous viewers

- More than one viewer simultaneously streaming live/recorded video from a streaming source (including PTZ)

- Ability to view video while also being a streaming source for other viewers

- The Streaming service will support smart packet duplication from the BE streaming server so that only one copy of the video is sent from the streaming source to the BE and the BE sends the required number of copies to the viewers.

Authorization/authentication filtering

- Authorization (login or role based) required to initiate a push/pull of video streams from on-system devices.

- Authorization required to access fixed surveillance camera via system API
- Authorization based on dynamic roles per incident (incident supervisor has higher rights than other responders)

Audit Log

- The Streaming Service shall support local audit logging of all streaming activity for both streaming source and streaming viewer applications.
- The Video Hub DVMS will log all streaming requests for stored DME

Fixed Surveillance APIs

- API will support an interface to an external Fixed Surveillance system that will support search/view of internal live streaming sources (Video Hub DVRs, Win mobile Handhelds)
- API will support an interface to an external Fixed Surveillance system that will support search/view of internal video storage locations (Video Hub DVR, Video Hub DVMS)
- Internal viewers (wired and wireless clients) can access/view external surveillance cameras via Surveillance API
- Internal viewers (wired and wireless clients) can access/view external video stored in a NVR database via Surveillance API.
- API should be based on a standards based NNI protocol
- Video Hub Viewers will only support viewing video from surveillance cameras/systems that support the following video/audio encoding formats.
  - Video: MPEG-4 SP; H.264 BP or MP (no B-frames); MJPEG; MPEG-2
  - Audio: AAC-LC or H.726
- Additional error resiliency for streaming of surveillance video will not be supported by Video Hub Streaming service for R1.0
- The bit rate of the surveillance system will be the bit rate utilized by the Video Hub Streaming Service

Presence

- A directory of internal live video streaming sources shall be available to all streaming end users
- A directory of external live video streaming sources shall be available to all streaming end users

- A directory of all video streaming viewers shall be available to all streaming end users

- A directory of active streaming sessions shall be available to all streaming end users

- Directory should include real time information including device location and device status.

  - Timing interval for status updates should be customer configurable and should support a minimum update time of 1 minute.

  - System shall be designed so that shift changes do not overwhelm the network with Presence updates.

- A search/query functionality shall be available to assist users in finding desired streaming sources

- A filtering functionality should be provided so that subset of the directory are seen by users based on

  - Location; areas of patrol coverage

    - Basic square delineation - preconfigured

  - Security Permissions

  - Role in organization

- A mapping or location based function should be available to assist in selecting streaming sources of interest.

  - For mobile streaming sources, there will be some latency associated with the update of the information to the UI based upon the timing interval configured by the admin at system set up.

- Publish a directory of internal live video sources to external system

Session Control/Arbitration

- The Streaming Service shall provide an arbitration/control mechanism that will ensure that only one viewer at a time can PTZ control an internal or external camera

- The Streaming Service shall support a centralized session control/arbitration functionality that is configurable based on user role, user associated with streaming source, or user associated with initial streaming request

- The Streaming Service shall support functionality to allow transfer of streaming control based on request from a streaming participant and acceptance from session control leader

- The Streaming Service will support functionality to allow the streaming source to gracefully terminate streaming sessions on a stream-by-stream basis

- The Streaming Service shall support the establishment of a Video Director role who will have the ability to direct the selection of viewing sources and viewing angles (PTZ) for a group of viewers

Search/Query

- A user can search via the Streaming Application, video stored in a Video Hub DVMS database. The video can then be selected and streamed to the user or to other viewers as selected by the user

- A user can search via the Streaming Application, video stored on a remote Video Hub IV-DVR HDD. The video can then be selected and streamed to the user or to other viewers as selected by the user

- A user can search via the Streaming Application, video stored in an external Video Surveillance System. The video can then be selected and streamed to the user or to other viewers as selected by the user

- Internal viewers can query external NVR databases for recorded video streams.

Security

- End-to-end encryption at the application layer is not required.

- Network encryption will be provided by the customer VPN or other customer encryption mechanism

8. THE UNIFIED RECORD MANAGEMENT SYSTEM

The Unified Record Management System (URMS) is a self creating data store that provides the traditional benefits of a relational model without requiring a prior understanding of the users data needs. URMS is a standardized approach for data storage regardless of the complexity of the data and allows for automatic extensibility and complete flexibility for any stored document. In the URMS a document is not a reference to a particular format for the data but the context or boundary of that data. URMS fundamentally approaches data storage from data boundaries and data use. Each data boundary is optimized for the functionality it provides. URMS creates four fundamental boundaries based upon four abstracted data needs:

- o Understanding the Data
- o Consuming the Data
- o Finding the Data
- o Analyzing the Data

The URMS is part of the Platform Services offered by the Unified Intelligent Video Analytics Suite. Other components may use the URMS for storage of suite documents or external documents.

The URMS consists of four logical data stores that are consistent with the fundamental data boundaries described in the introduction. Each of the logical data stores are abstracted and optimized to enable the data use designated in its boundary. Each logical data store includes a service that acts as an entry point. The four logical data stores are the following:

- Metadata Store

- Document Store

- Index Store

- Analysis Store

The high level architecture of the URMS is shown below.

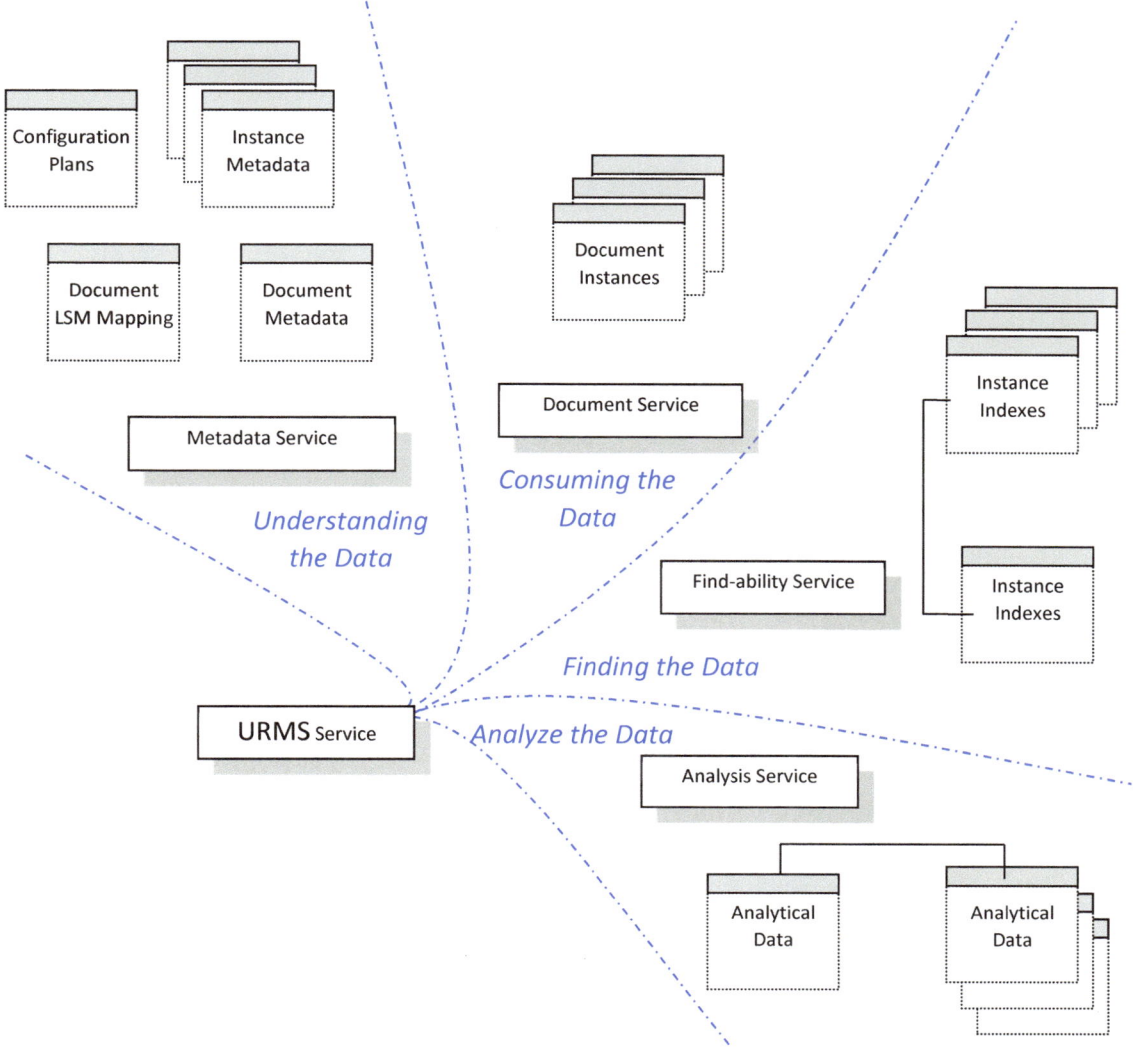

All four logical data stores have a service that is provides the transaction capabilities against its store. Any time a transaction crosses multiple boundaries the URMS Service will be used and will act as a coordinator between each of the logical data store services. All configurations will pass through the URMS Service because any configuration can affect multiple logical data Stores. Configuration is done as any document is registered in the URMS and for the initial install. Configuration can be made available for the customer through the provisioning console.

All configurations will be plan based and the configuration will be executed either immediately or by a preconfigured execution date. All configuration plans will be saved in the Metadata Store and can be used for by support to determine current configuration or can be used to roll back data store to a prior configuration.

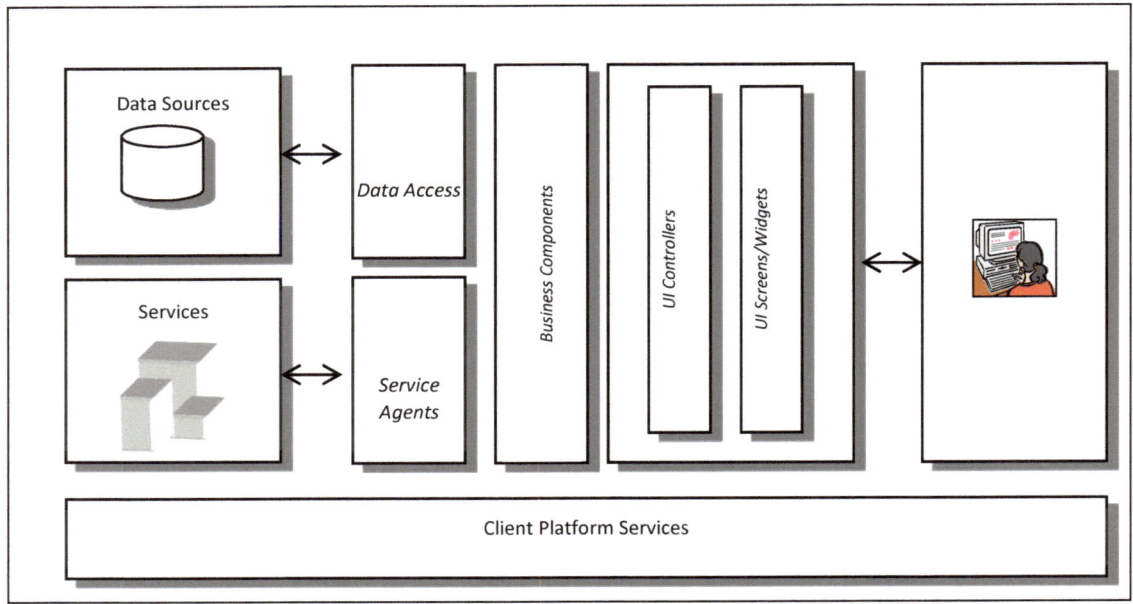

The URMS provides "thin" clients that can be built upon to create specific client application. The Client Frameworks defined for the URMS provides best practices patterns that can be leveraged by the Product Development Teams. Specific clients will follow this basic architecture with implementations that meet their specific needs. As development progresses, if it is found that an implementation can be leveraged across multiple clients, then that architecture will be adopted as a "common architecture" and further described in future revisions of this document.

The Client Architecture Framework specifies a layered architecture composed of multiple components following industry best practices and patterns. The layers defined within the Framework include:

- User Screens/Widgets
- User Controller
- Action Engine
- Business Components
- Service Agents
- Data Access Logic Components
- Security Management

For the Clients, the Common UI Framework defines the use of the Model-View-Controller (MVC) pattern. The MVC pattern is an industry best practice that provides for the separation of the control portion of the application from its presentation and data. The components of it are:

- Application **model**, with its data representation and business logic
- **Views** that provide data presentation and user input
- **Controller** to dispatch requests and control the application flow.

This separation enables applications display to be readily changed without effecting the underlying control and data of the application. In addition, it facilitates the sharing of the business objects between multiple interfaces.

The Handler receives all web page requests. Based on its configuration information, the Request Handler maps the page request to a specific Command Processors. The Command Processors implement a standard interface with the Handler but are application specific and implemented by the application developer. The Command Processor Components will access the necessary business logic components to complete their tasks.

Once the Action Classes receives the data necessary to render the next "page", it passes the data to the "View" components of the MVC pattern. The "View" components are application specific and can be implemented in a number of ways including ASP pages or XSLT transforms. In either case, the "View" components take the input data and output a "page" for the thin client browser to display.

Localization and globalization enables the application views to be customized for a specific language and/or region. In order to support this application "text" strings and images are separated into resource files for each language or region. For a given deployment, the appropriate resource files are provisioned to support the language required. The individual ASP "pages" of the application refer to the provisioned resource file in order to retrieve the desired text strings and/or images. As a result, the configuration of a new language does not impact the rest of the application presentation or the business logic and data.

Multiple languages can be supported via the user selection. For example, a user can select the language in which they want the UI to be presented.

9. THE PLATFORM

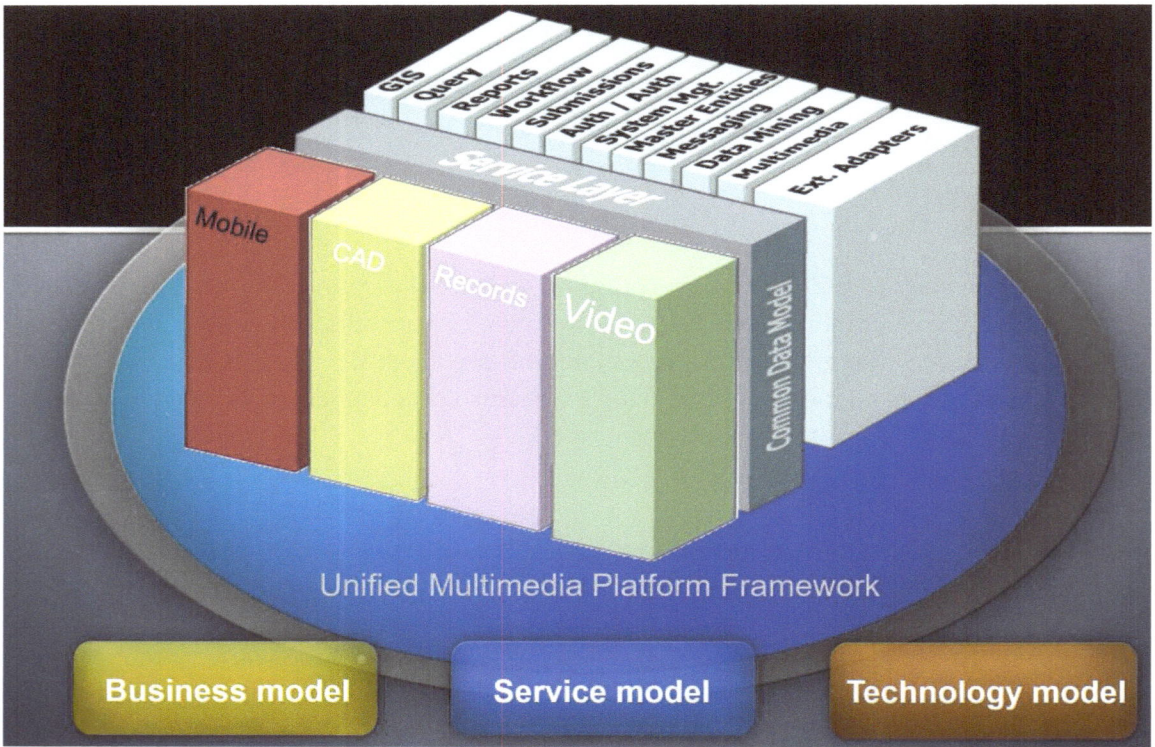

Our vision focuses on the continuity of experience across the traditional seams that can occur when devices, locations, networks and services change. The Unified Suite builds on that vision by breaking down the seams between traditional multimedia management products and the seams between wired and wireless access to multimedia information.

The Unified Suite stresses integration of functionality and information across product boundaries. This focus on seamless integration starts with a commitment to common technology components. For us, this means a single development environment. For a customer this means this entire suite is deployed on the same type of server, runs the same operating system and uses the same underlying database system. System administration tools are common across the Suite. This standardization eases administration and maintenance for both our company and Unified Suite customers. Seamless integration is a key business driver of the Unified Suite Services Oriented Architecture (SOA), in which individual features and functionality of the applications will be exposed to each other and to external systems as services. At a high level, the suite architecture is divided into multiple layers and slices.

To addressing market segmentation, the Unified Suite must be highly configurable to cost effectively adapt to the different needs of customers using the same standard COTS release. Configuration in the Unified Suite falls under several broads areas:

➢ Operation, Administration, and Maintenance
  Configurable settings that allow an administrator to manage and monitor the execution of the system. Application Management, System Monitoring, Fault Management, Audit Management, Configuration Management, Archive/Backup/Restore, Scheduling, Diagnostics Management, Performance Management, etc.

➢ Security
  Includes authentication and authorization and various configurable security policies.

➢ Suite Provisioning
  Defining Groups, Users, Roles, Devices, etc., including hierarchical relationships. Also includes supplying the data for the various lists, codes and statutes used by the Suite

➢ Application Provisioning
  Defines application behaviors – typically the type of behaviors that can be selected from a predefined list. Also includes the configuration of the various types of geographic information used by the suite (maps, layers, etc.)

Extended

It is impractical to include all the possible 'configurations' to address all markets and every possible customer. This is the driving reason for the concept of extension and customization.

Extensions are 'additive' in nature. For instance, additional fields, additional forms, and additional reports are common in a records context. Additional commands and unique interface transactions are common in a context. Adding an extension does not require modification to code that makes up the base product. The Unified Suite facilitates extensions to allow more competitive answers to functional requirements. Detailed rules for what are (and are not) an extensions will be defined as part of the sales support process. For instance, information (data) added to an application may not break the relational structure or transaction business logic of the core functions in the product to which it is being added.

Unified Suite extensions are generally managed by specific tools. For example, additional forms are created by using a Unified Suite Forms Editor tool. Custom Reports are created using Crystal Reports. Extensions will usually be provided by our professional services. However, as Unified Suite tools mature, trained customers and 3rd parties will also be able to extend the product.

Customization

Some customer requirements cannot be met by configuration or extension. The type of functionality requested requires change to the core code that makes up the Unified Suite. This level of customization requires that the resulting deliverables always be treated as customer specific builds. There are two levels of this type of customization to consider:

➢ Pure customization refers to a customer specific project that may (or may not) use some of the existing assets of the Unified Suite as a one-time starting point to construct the desired system. The resultant system is not a new version of Unified Suite -- it is effectively a new and separate product. Roadmaps are not aligned. Components are not shared and future modifications to one system do not impact the other. A business that chooses to do pure customization must be organized to minimize the impact to the COTS product resources, roadmap, and technology choices. Unified Suite Customization Continuum does not include pure customization as part of the Unified Suite support as all of the development and support activities occur outside of the Unified Suite program.

➢ Of more direct impact to the Unified Suite program is the potential to enable developers (Company, Customer, 3rd party) to modify and/or replace core components of Unified Suite in order to meet specific customer requirements without breaking the link to the Unified Suite roadmap, support, and future enhancements. This type of customization requires well described services, APIs, sophisticated software development kits (SDK), developer support, testing/certification programs, and other policies to manage the complexity inherent in allowing the Unified Suite to provide supported, long-lived, components to diverse development teams. The resultant systems are a derivative version of the Unified Suite. The incremental modification is supported as customer specific components but future Unified Suite enhancements can be used by the derivative system assuming the developers followed all of the compatibility, standards and practice rules. In essence, this type of customization builds on the additive concept of extension by enabling replacement and/or modification of certain core components – but is at a considerably more complex, object oriented and service isolated level. The Unified Suite will explore this type of customization in future releases to enable tailored solutions for customers with unique requirements without incurring the costs of pure customization.

Our multimedia fusion framework with service coordination and orchestration capabilities, not only for services that are built on top of the platform but also for 3rd party services, applications, as well as legacy functions, with a coherent set of analytical functions to fully support automated and scalable decision making capabilities (i.e., through the government of dynamic, situation-aware policies):

- *A Single Unified Platform:* The unified process offers a ubiquitous, service oriented solution for public security system across all public security domains. Unified SOA and business process management makes all integration modules participate in end-to-end governance and management through integration with multimedia repository and SOA Management. Its integration seamlessly integrates with multimedia to service-enable public security business processes to be flexible enough to meet the evolving demands of requirements.
- *Multimedia Fusion:* The multimedia data services management platform is for building Information-as-a-Service (IaaS) deployments. It transforms heterogeneous, siloed multimedia data into reusable information services providing real-time, accurate information to people, processes, and applications. It also includes technology for the complete information-services life cycle, including ingestion, archiving, indexing, analysis, retrieval, dispatch, and management.
- *Dynamic Service Orchestration:* Public security organizations need to leverage the existing applications, but also expand their capabilities by transforming them into services in order to drive new levels of customer service and move quickly into dynamic situations/environments. They need services distributed across multiple

public security domains to build high-value composite applications. The integration framework unifies and simplifies their efforts to integrate all systems, applications, and data sources to get tangible results. It ensures investment protection in existing applications and infrastructure now and into the future.

- *Security Management:* Let only the right people to access the right information in the right place at the right time.

Our products provide the flexibility and interoperability required in dynamic assembly and coordination of services, which commonly involve massively distributed components, legacy systems, and diverse technologies. Moreover, we fully integrate process logic with decision logic, and we take into account the local autonomies and address the need for distributed decision making in service composition and orchestration. Our system delivers demand driven, integrated, and personalized services through dynamic service creation and orchestration. Our policy-based adaptive behavior orchestration solution can be used to tackle these problems and provide a fully distributed and scalable solution. It is designed to offer an extensible and pluggable framework with an external and independent control point, allowing distributed decision making to be completely automated and integrated with process management.

Our Unified Intelligent Video Analytics Suite provides different products to automatically and intelligently extract critical information from videos and cameras for a variety of purposes, and manage all those information, videos and cameras. It is a combination of imaging, computer vision, pattern analysis, and machine intelligence applied to real-world problems. Its utility spans several industry segments including video surveillance, retail, and transportation. Video analytics is distinct from machine vision or machine inspection and is similar to automotive vision. Some applications of analytics include the detection of suspicious objects and activities for offering better security, in license plate recognition and traffic analysis for intelligent transportation systems, and in customer counting and queue management for retail applications.

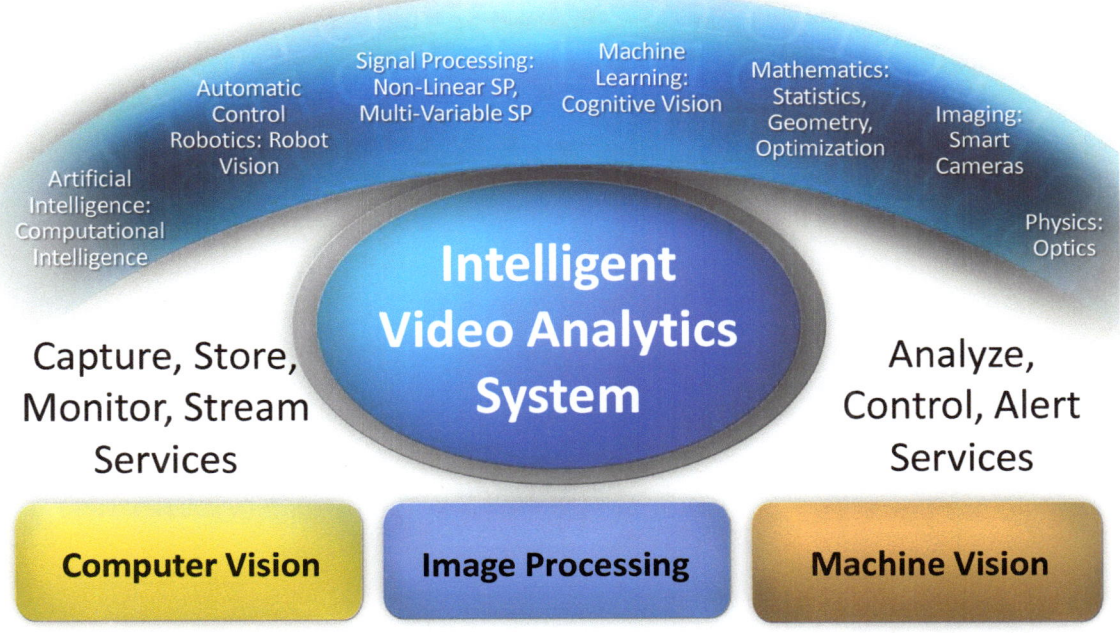

Not like other security and surveillance systems, we not only claim that our solution is one of the most "intelligent" system developed by the latest software engineering technologies, and with rich multimedia management capabilities on a scalable unified multimedia framework; but also, perhaps the more important, we help you do your business with most effectiveness and secure by our solution. First, our solution is an application of artificial intelligence; specifically, computer vision, a truly intelligent vision-based system. Second, our software system is capable of accurately separating foreground from background objects, creates a stream of metadata that reflects a 24/7 analysis of the view, interprets and reports on actual events, rather than just react to movement. Third, our system is able to provide the user with relevant real-time information about these events. It is able to help people easily and intelligently interact with the system in order to make the critical decisions. We have spent years of research and development time on video analytics and we are ready to commercially our video analytic capabilities to market.

Our video analytics suite uses a series of processing steps, composed of our unique algorithms with the latest software engineering technologies. The video processing pipeline is shown below. The processing steps are shown as rectangular blocks, which include segmentation, classification, tracking, and activity recognition. These processing blocks depend on models that can include a background model, a camera model, one or more appearance models, motion models, and shape models. These models are generally updated over time, with learning and adaptation being done over a series of frames. As frames progress through these processing steps, intermediate output results are produced which are shown in the bubbles in the top row. Multiple trackers and classifiers can run in parallel or run optionally based on the results of upstream processes and configuration.

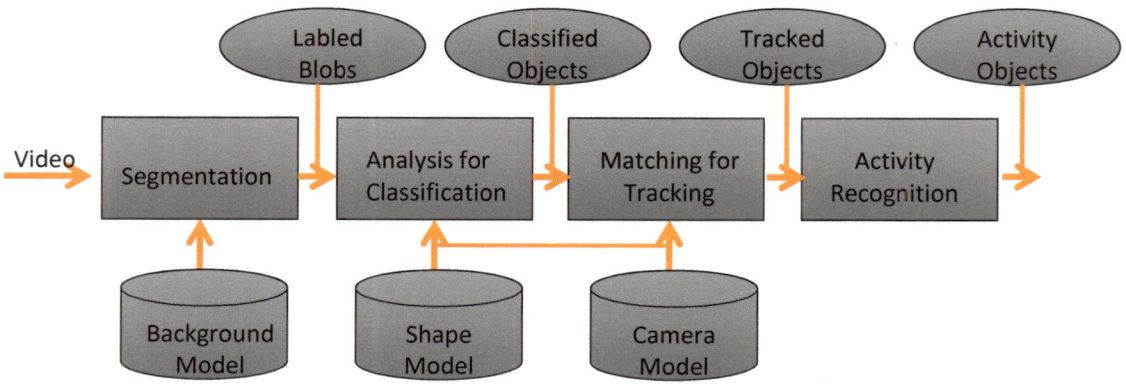

For example, in our fact detection algorithm, in the first step the system uses an adaptive pre-filter to eliminate candidate rectangles in the input that it can confidently determine do not contain faces. In the second step the system feeds the remaining rectangles to an improved implementation of the fact detection algorithm. Finally, in the third step the system attempts to eliminate false positives. It applies a color filter and an edge filter to improve the precision of the detection. It uses a support vector machine (SVM) filter, plus lighting correction and histogram equalization, to further eliminate false positives. The system then outputs each rectangle, which contains a detected face, along with its confidence in each detection.

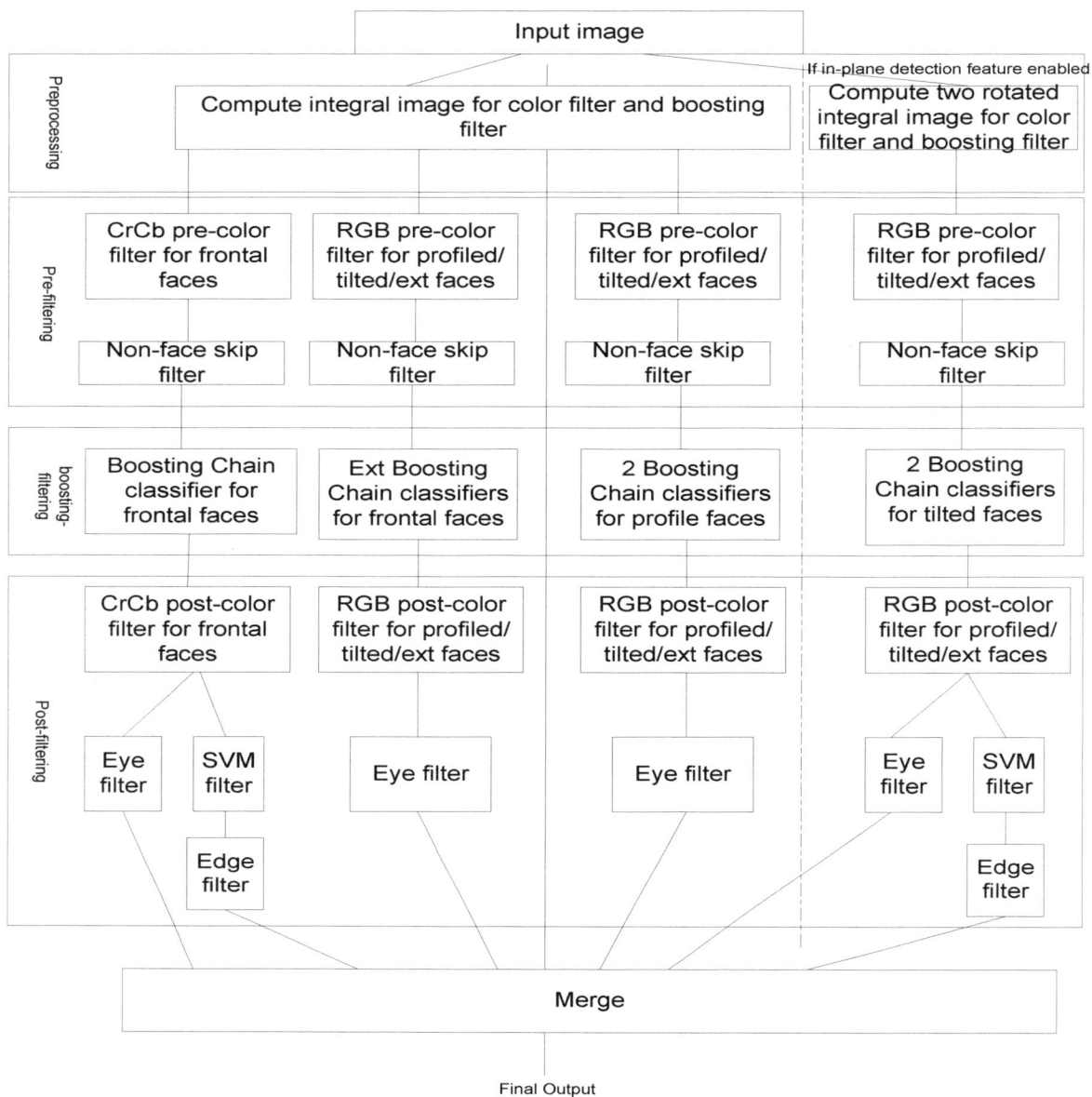

In order to simplify the face detection problem, the system divides the target faces to be detected into four categories: upright frontal face, extend frontal face set with difficulty illumination/lighting and expression, profiled face (left profile and right profile), and in-plane rotated face (clockwise and anti-clockwise). Three sets of filters are applied to each kind of face. After the filtering stage, regions detected are merged to generate final result.

Real time alerts

A lot of alerts are defined by our intelligent video surveillance system user. They are generic alerts, such as detecting an abandoned object or an item in the scene moving over a set speed limit. To trigger these alarms, only the properties of the object movements are analyzed by the system. More specific alerts can be issued after the objects or their movement have been classified (e.g., discrimination between the passage of a human or animal in an outside area). Behaviour-related alerts based on conformity or non-conformity with a behaviour model entered in the system (e.g., an individual trying to open more than one car in a parking lot), constitute pre-defined alerts.

Certain real-time alerts are automatically identified. Over time, our system learns a model of activity and ends up detecting non-standard activities. For example, it may learn that vehicles drive on the street and pedestrians walk on the sidewalk. The opposite may trigger an alarm.

Video search for investigation

Our analytics processing makes it possible to index video content based on characteristics such as the shape of objects, their size, appearance, trajectory, type, as well as their model of activity. Stored as metadata, this information makes it possible to conduct spatiotemporal searches such as "find all footage with a person dressed in red passing in front of a certain building between two given dates".

The analytical functions developed for our video surveillance systems have different levels of analysis. Hierarchically, they are executed at the pixel and object level to achieve the behaviour scale. They are grouped according to the following tasks:

➤ Detection of changes

Our video surveillance system, can detect changes in video footage. It may detect an activity in a scene under surveillance, in particular the movement of objects. It may also reveal the appearance or disappearance of an object (abandoned or stolen object). It is also used to automatically report accidental or intentional alterations in a camera: obstructions (dust, spider webs, moisture, paint, stickers), reorientation, blurriness.

Our patented technique for detecting movements used in video analytics are not only based on detecting changes, moreover, detecting changes in video footage does not specifically target the movement of objects, but may highlight an image modulation. In order to segment moving objects, it is be able to discriminate between fluctuations in pixel value corresponding to consistent movements and fluctuations caused by environmental changes.

Even in complex environments that may present many, sometimes sudden variations: change in lighting (shadows, movement of the sun, clouds, mirror reflections in glass or on water, glare caused by sources of light in the scene), non-relevant movements (flag flapping in the wind, waves on water), our analytical methods work well. Our algorithms that are robust enough to be applied in uncontrolled settings.

➤ Segmentation of moving objects

Subtraction of the background: In its most primitive form, detecting changes comes down to finding, pixel by pixel, differences in colour or texture between the images of a sequence. A first category of techniques consists in comparing each frame of a sequence to a reference image, called the background, which represents the undisturbed scene. The areas of change are formed of pixels with a difference in intensity that is above a threshold. Pixel-by-pixel subtraction between two images is very sensitive to the slightest environmental change, such as changes in lighting and movements inherent to a scene (e.g., the foliage of a tree blowing in the wind). In order to offset this problem, certain techniques continually adapt the background model to intrinsic changes in the environment. The difference with the background is a method that is particularly suited to indoor environments, where lighting conditions are controlled and where there is little activity (e.g., monitoring a hallway).

Time-based difference: A second class of methods for detecting change is based on a time difference between a few consecutive frames. These frames adapt to variations in the time of the environment. On the other hand, they tend to oversee certain variations related to the movement of objects in the scene, especially if they move slowly. They often produce holes in the objects detected. These techniques therefore require smoothing treatment, with morphological operators and filtering of holes and shapes that are too small. In order to retain only significant movements and eliminate occasional movements, certain techniques draw up a map of the regions with a high level of activity, based on a movement pattern.

Optical Flow: Methods that analyze optical flow help to detect consistent directions of pixel change associated with the movement of objects in the scene. However, they require complex calculations that are difficult to do in real time. Optical flow is also sensitive to the image's noise.

➢ Monitoring of objects

After detecting moving objects, intelligent video surveillance systems track their movement over the video footage. Each task requires locating each object tracked from one image to another. This can be done in 2D with a single camera, or in 3D combining two views with known geometric relationship.

Many tracking techniques are based on mathematical methods that make it possible to predict an object's position on a frame based on its movement in the previous frames. Tracking several objects at the same time poses many challenges. Each object detected in a frame must be associated with its corresponding object in the subsequent frame. This matching is done based on the objects' outlines, their characteristics (e.g., corners, area, ratios, etc.), or their model of appearance.

Occlusions (regions hidden by others) represent a major difficulty for tracking objects. A video surveillance system may lose track of an object if it is totally or partially obstructed over a certain period of time. It may also be difficult to separate two objects when they are very close or when one hides another.

➢ Classification and identification of objects

Objects detected by a video surveillance system are usually classified into different categories: human, vehicle, animal, etc. This classification may be done prior to tracking in order to retain only the trajectories of objects that are relevant for surveillance purposes.

In general, systems recognize the nature of an entity detected based on its shape attributes and movement properties. For example, a human is usually presented as a form that is taller than it is wide, whereas an automobile would be wider than it is tall. Human gait has specific features, in particular, a certain periodicity.

Object identification pushes recognition further. After finding the class to which an object belongs, it must be identified. With surveillance, and in particular for access control or when searching for a suspect, the goal is to recognize an individual or decipher a vehicle license plate. Vast research and development efforts have been invested in recent years in these two specialized applications.

Recognizing human faces and gait are the two main biometric tools to identify people in video surveillance. Analysis of gait provides clues for the preliminary identification of an individual filmed from a distance, in a wide field.

Face recognition provides for a more accurate identification, but requires a face image with good resolution and in a proper position (facing forward as much as possible). Most methods will tolerate a face rotation of up to 45°. Many face encoding and comparison techniques have been proposed since the early 90s and are based primarily on the extraction of mathematical descriptors or topological points on the face. Initially developed based on photographs, face recognition applications have existed for a few years on video footage. Depending on the method used, recognition can be achieved by changing appearance, such as the addition of glasses or a beard, facial expressions and lighting. New 3D face recognition techniques appear to improve identification performance and robustness in comparison to 2D techniques. However, face recognition in an uncontrolled environment, such as a crowd, continues to be a problem that has not yet been satisfactorily resolved by current video analytics systems.

Reading license plates from video surveillance is a difficult application. It requires a high-resolution image. There are many environmental interferences when analyzing an image: bad weather, headlight brightness, dirty or damaged plate. In order to read a license plate, a system must first locate the rectangle of the plate among all of the image's details. It must then proceed with optical character recognition. A plate filmed at an angle distorts the characters in the image and complicates the recognition process. In order to maximize the system's efficiency, plate recognition is done most often using specialized systems that concentrate on camera positioning and lighting quality.

➢ Classification of activities and behaviours

One of the goals of video surveillance is to interpret the individual behaviours of the objects in a scene and their interactions. Broadly speaking, behaviours are defined as the observable actions of agents (humans, animals, vehicles, etc.) Since behaviour recognition requires a semantic, sometimes complex analysis of what appears in the image, it is the most difficult challenge for video analytics systems.

The goal may be to detect a simple behaviour, such as "an individual has left a bag in a room." However, the chain of interactions may quickly become complex: Individual A leaves a bag in a room. Individual B takes the bag and leaves the room. Individual B bumps into individual A and shakes his hand. Conclusion: the bag was not stolen.

Analyzing and interpreting behaviours means recognizing movement patterns and extracting from them, at a higher level, a description of the actions and interactions. As is the case with all classification issues, a sequence of characteristics observed has to be associated with a model sequence representing a specific behaviour. The problem therefore consists of modelling typical behaviours, by learning or by definition, and finding a comparison method that tolerates slight variations.

Hidden Markov Models, neural networks and Bayesian networks are among the most used techniques for modelling normal behaviour and detecting deviant behaviour. These techniques trigger an alarm based on statistical discrepancy with the inferred model of the scene. Predefined event detection methods also exist. These are based on a system of rules, such as triggering an alarm if an object bigger than a threshold value remains stationary for a certain period of time in a given region.

➢ Crowd Analysis

A domain of the future in video analytics research is crowd analysis and monitoring. With the quick escalation of the global population, the densification of large urban centres, and the growing issue of providing security during large gatherings, video surveillance has become an interesting avenue. Cameras are actually already set up to monitor large events (such as sporting events, political conventions, etc.), but the analytical efficiency of video systems in this context remains debatable.

Estimating density is a fundamental step in crowd monitoring and management, requiring an approximate assessment of the number of individuals. The numerous occlusions and juxtapositions make pedestrian segmentation for counting purposes difficult. Some techniques assume a proportional relationship between the number of pixels associated with the foreground, following segmentation, and the number of people. Other methods are based on image texture in order to characterize crowd density. Certain algorithms detect head contour, while others use the histograms of several characteristics to deduce the approximate number of people.

Although object tracking is one of the most popular research topics in video surveillance, most of the algorithms developed apply to a small number of people (less than ten at a time). Tracking pedestrians in crowds presents major difficulties, especially with respect to the large number of individuals to be followed from one frame to the next and the numerous occlusions present. Some methods track key features, which are less subject to being disturbed by occlusions than contours. Others model the human body or its parts. Probabilistic matching methods or specific filters are used to follow these models during video footage.

It is important to follow a crowd's movements for security purposes. For example, the crowd's trajectory and flow will be analyzed. When modelling the crowd and its behaviours, certain researchers consider the crowd as a whole and interpret the movements of the different parts. Techniques such as optical flow and hidden Markov models are used to model movements. Some models will combine microscopic (individual) and macroscopic (crowd) analysis. In this context, two types of approaches are proposed to describe a crowd's activity: the application of physical models, such as the kinematics of gas particles and fluid dynamics, and agent-based techniques.

➤ Active Video Surveillance in Multi-Camera Systems

Modern video surveillance systems, in particular on IP networks, may be comprised of hundreds of cameras. Sometimes, several cameras cover the same area. Some of them are power-operated and can be controlled to capture further details on an event detected in a wide field. For example, the camera can zoom in on an individual penetrating an area in order to identify him/her. In certain networks, cameras are intelligent, i.e., they have their own processing unit. They can exchange information with a central system or directly amongst themselves.

These surveillance camera networks make it possible to follow objects over extensive areas. Furthermore, multiple views may help to solve object occlusion problems. In a distributed architecture, analytical processing can be done in parallel, thereby accelerating the analysis and saving on bandwidth by transmitting only metadata.

However, these networks also raise specific problems that the scientific world is trying to solve:

✓ Camera calibration: Operation that consists in establishing a correspondence between the global reference mark of the scene observed and the camera coordinate system, as well as in determining the camera's intrinsic parameters, such as distortion. This precision process may be tedious for a network with many cameras. It is preferable to develop analytical functions that do not require any camera calibration or self-calibrating methods.

✓ Movement detection: For a power-operated camera, the camera's movement creates an apparent change in the image. Movement detection methods must distinguish between camera movement and independent changes.

✓ Object tracking on several cameras: In order to be able to track an object from one camera to the next, correspondence must be established between the different views in a common reference point. Camera resetting consists in calculating parameters for transforming the image from one camera to the next based on the change in reference point and the movement model. This operation uses a priori knowledge of the scene's topology. It allows for an increased 2D (2D1/2) or 3D view to be obtained of the scene. Changes in object appearance and positioning over time, as well as changes in lighting, complicate the resetting process.

✓ Detection of camera tampering: The more cameras a network has, the more difficult it is to control how they function. These systems must have built-in tools for automatic detection of camera breakdowns and alterations in order to remain functional.

Multi-camera active video surveillance systems are used above all for monitoring extensive or distributed areas, such as transportation systems, banking infrastructures, government institutions (military bases, prisons, strategic infrastructures, radar centres, hospitals), public buildings, shopping malls and parking lots.

11. VIDEO RECORDING AND STORAGING LEVEL SERVICES

This recording feature is the core capability of our recording function to save A/V and Metadata (M) content to persistent storage (disk). The "track" terminology is used to refer to a "recording session" from a A/V/M source (as much as possible, a "track" is treated virtually). Also, no assumptions are made with regards to the type of media encoder used, nor underlying filesystem or file layout, but it is assumed that media content and Metadata are recorded, can be cross-referenced, and retrieved.

This search feature is the ability to search A/V content and return desired content, based upon certain criteria. The criteria can simply be time range of content capture and/or content source designation. More advanced criteria would encompass searching A/V content based upon Metadata (Events) that can be cross-referenced to the A/V content. For example, Intrusion Detection or Fire Alarm may generate an Event, which the Recorder has subscribed to. The Recorder saves the Event and can associate that Event with A/V content using timestamps. The user can then perform an advanced search based upon Intrusion Detection Events and receive A/V content associated with all Intrusion Detection Events, or narrowed further by time ranges.

1	Basic	Records: Video	Records Video content
2	Full	Records: Audio	Records Audio content
3	Full	Records: Metadata	Stores Metadata for playback with A/V content or by itself. Metadata broadly refers to Events or Alarms, the source of which can be Visual Motion Detection, Video Analytics, Point of Sale transaction, Intrusion Alarm, Fire Alarm, Entry Access Event, User Event, etc.
4	Full	Event-triggered recording	This is a more advanced recording mode (vs #5). This feature refers to the ability to begin recording A/V content based on a reception of an Event or Alarm. A track is typically configured to record either continuously (#5) or Event-triggered (#4). A special case is the "Manually controlled" track, which starts/stops recording only based upon a specifically defined command to do so.
5	Basic	Continuous recording	This is a basic recording mode. Once the track is started, it will record all Audio, Video, or Metadata content from a source, until it's allocated track space is full. (If #9 is enabled, then recording will

			continue in a circular fashion at the beginning of the track's allocated spce.)
6	Optio nal	Schedule-based recording	This feature refers to the ability to alter the recording mode (#4 / #5) based upon a time of day or day of week. Schedule applies to continuous or event-based recording
7	Full	Pre/Post-Event recording buffer	This is a basic (configurable) attribute of Event-triggered recording. Before any event is received, the recorder continuously maintains a buffer queue of A/V content (in memory) in anticipation of future event reception. When the recorder receives an Event that is configured to trigger recording, it will "commit" the Pre-Event buffer in memory to persistent storage (disk), and, then, continue to commit "live" content to storage, until a configured Post-Event buffer time or size quota is achieved.
8	Optio nal	Event-based recording policy changes	This is an advanced feature similar to #6, except that the changes to the recording mode are based on Event/Alarm reception. #6 & #8, when combined, and with the addition of a "Rules Engine" can provide more sophisticated recording capability. In addition to recording mode changes, the quality of recording content can also be changed (e.g. Modify recording quality, resolution or fps on event).
9	Basic	Recording Loop Enable/Disable	Ability to specify whether the recorder can loop back to beginning of a track when it reaches end of allocated disk space.
10	Basic	Playback: Recorded Video	At correct rate
11	Full	Playback: Recorded Audio	At correct rate (If recorded, should be playable)
12	Full	Playback: Recorded Metadata	At correct rate (If recorded, should be playable)
13	Optional	PlaybackTrick-Mode on Server: FF	Fast-forward (i.e. "Scale:" > 1.0, with "Speed:" >= 1)
	Optional	Playback Trick-Modes on Server: FR	Fast-rewind (i.e. "Scale:" < -1.0, with "Speed:" >= 1)
	Optional	Playback Trick-Modes on Server: Pause	Pause (wait without discarding data, RTSP PAUSE supports this.)
	Optional	Playback Trick-Modes on Server: Step	Step frame by frame (i.e. sequence of Play with "Range:")

14	Optional	Dynamic media-stream property changes	Server (and Client) supports changing stream properties during playback.
15	Optional	Playback scalability	Playback at different scalability profile (spatial or temporal). For example, request only I-frames or a lower spatial resolution. This is a server-side feature, meaning that the client can always pre-buffer content (then thin) to provide this feature.
16	Basic	Search media by source	Requires identification of source by name or number.
17	Full	Search media by property	Resolution, FPS, quality, bit-rate, etc.
18	Basic	Search media by time/date	Time/date ranges
19	Full	Search media by event/alarm	As defined in #3
20	Full	Search media by motion	Simple VMD
21	Optional	Search media by analytics	More advanced Audio and Video Analytics. Note that, in general, this refers to Event tagging of "live" Video/Autio content by an Analytics engine as the content stream is received. Further, more intensive, post-recording, A/V Analytics can be done for the purposes of content searching, but that is certainly not a required feature.
22	Optional	Search media by other metadata	(e.g. Location for mobile sources)
23	Optional	Search media by wildcard	Allow wildcard or regular expression matching on search fields.
24	Optional	Advanced Searching	Intelligent searching rules, filtering, previewing, etc.
25	Optional	Transfer to remote client	Ability to pull content over a reliable transport link or the ability to push content to another network client (alternate method to RTSP/RTP Playback mechanisms).
26	Optional	Transfer to remote client or alternate storage based on schedule or policy	Advanced feature (e.g. push content to another node based on time of day or day of week or Event/Alarm.)
27	Optional	Transfer bandwidth management	Ability to control bandwidth used for transfers (this may also be related to flow control and protocol selection). This is both a network friendliness feature (i.e. avoid congesting

			the network during large, bulk transfers) and transfer reliability feature (e.g. set QoS / DCSP during transfers).
28	Optional	Transfer interrupt / resume	Ability to interrupt/resume a transfer
29	Full	Configure Track size by recording time	Requires knowledge of expected recording bit-rate, or ability to grow allowable track size dynamically based on data rate.
30	Basic	Configure Track size by disk allocation (GB)	
31	Full	Configure Track size by % of total	
32	Full	Content Locking / Protection	Ability to mark/unmark content, by time range, as protected from removal.
33	Full	Content Thinning/Pruning: age-based	"In-place" deletion of older content. "In-place" refers to deletion of data in the recorders persistent storage (disk) vs. discarding or filtering during transfer to another level of storage.
34	Optional	Content Thinning/Pruning: other policy based algorithms	Prune based on rules. e.g. temporal filtering, or auto delete after moving to 2nd tier storage.
35	Full	Content Integrity Checking	Can be simple chkdsk or codec aware data validation (corruption detection). May also include watermarking or the ability to detect content tampering.

12. Video Analytics Protocol Specification for Event and Metadata Output

In our suite, from a technical perspective, we use the Video Analytics Protocol (or "VAP"), which defines a common protocol using XML over HTTP/HTTPS. This protocol is similar in nature to Web services but is geared towards lightweight computing requirements on the device. As such, this uses a simplified XML schema. In addition, the VAP protocol treats all configuration and management aspects as resources utilizing the REpresentational State Transfer (REST) architecture.

REST Overview

REST is an approach to creating a service that exposes all information as resources in a uniform way. This approach is quite different from the traditional Remote Procedure Call (RPC) mechanism which identifies the functions that an application can call. Put simply, a REST Web application is noun-driven while an RPC Web application is verb-driven. For example, if a Web application were to define an RPC API for user management, it might be written as follows:

```
GET http://webserver/getUserList
GET http://webserver/getUser?userid=100
POST http://webserver/addUser
POST http://webserver/updateUser
GET http://webserver/deleteUser?userid=100
```

On the other hand, a REST API for the same operations would appear as follows:

```
GET http://webserver/users
GET http://webserver/users/user100
POST http://webserver/users
PUT http://webserver/users/user100
DELETE http://webserver/users/user100
```

Part of the simplicity of REST is its uniform interface for operations. Since everything is represented as a resource, create, retrieve, update, and delete (CRUD) operations use the same URI.

The CRUD operations are defined by the HTTP method as shown in the table below.

HTTP Method	Operation
POST	Create the resource
GET	Retrieve the resource
PUT	Update the resource
DELETE	Delete the resource

All GET calls will never change the system state. They only return data to the requestor and will not have side effects.

The following table shows how the HTTP status codes map to REST operations along with the general use case for response headers and bodies. For more information, please see the table under each REST API.

HTTP	REST Meaning	POST	GET	PUT	DEL
200	"OK" - The request has succeeded. Header Notes: None Body Notes: The requested resource will be returned in the body.		X	X	
201	"Created" - The request has created a new resource. Header Notes: The *Location* header contains the URI of the newly created resource. Body Notes: The response returns an entity describing the newly created resource.	X			
204	"No Content" - The request succeeded, but there is no data to return. Header Notes: None Body Notes: No body is allowed.			X	X
301	"Moved Permanently" - The requested resource has moved permanently. Header Notes: The *Location* header contains the URI of the new location. Body Notes: The body may contain the new resource location.		X		
302	"Found" - The requested resource should be accessed through this location, but the resource actually lives at another location. This is typically used to set up an alias. Header Notes: The *Location* header contains the URI of the resource. Body Notes: The body may contain the new resource location.		X		
400	"Bad Request" - The request was badly formed. This is commonly used for creating or updating a resource, but the data was incomplete or incorrect. Header Notes: The Reason-Phrase sent with the HTTP status header may contain information on the error. Body Notes: The response may contain more information of the underlying error that occurred in addition to the Reason-Phrase.	X		X	
401	"Unauthorized" - The request requires user authentication to access this resource. If the request contains invalid authentication data, this code is sent. Header Notes: At least one authentication mechanism must be specified in the *WWW-Authenticate* header. The Reason-Phrase sent with the HTTP status header may contain information on the error. Body Notes: The response may contain more information of the underlying error that occurred in addition to the Reason-Phrase.	X	X	X	X

HTTP	REST Meaning	POST	GET	PUT	DEL
403	"Forbidden" - The request is not allowed because the server is refusing to fill the request. A common reason for this is that the device does not support the requested functionality. Header Notes: The Reason-Phrase sent with the HTTP status header may contain information on the error. Body Notes: The response may contain more information of the underlying error that occurred in addition to the Reason-Phrase.	X	X	X	X
404	"Not Found" - The requested resource does not exist. Header Notes: None Body Notes: None	X	X	X	X
405	"Method Not Allowed" – The request used an HTTP method that is not supported for the resource because the VAP specification does not allow this method. If the device does not support the functionality but it is a valid VAP operation, then a 403 is returned. Header Notes: The *Allow* header lists the supported HTTP methods for this resource. Body Notes: None	X	X	X	X
500	"Internal Server Error" - An internal server error has occurred. Header Notes: None Body Notes: None	X	X	X	X
503	"Service Unavailable" – The HTTP server is up, but the REST service is not available. Typically this is caused by too many client requests. Header Notes: The *Retry-After* header suggests to the client when to try resubmitting the request. Body Notes: None	X	X	X	X

VAP REST APIs

This section details the VAP REST APIs. It is divided into the following sections:

- ➢ Protocol information
- ➢ Device information and configuration
- ➢ Channel information
- ➢ Alerts and counts

Each section contains a table listing the APIs supported and an XML snippet providing details on the XML format. The schema for the XML is provided alongside this document but there are some general guidelines. In the URI column, the URI is rooted as specified in the OVReadyProtocol (OV – Object Video) definition in the ovready.xml document, but the remainder of the URI must be used as it appears in the table.

In addition, VAP enables applications to determine the device capabilities by querying each device. This allows an application to adjust itself according to supported features.

1) Unique Identifiers

Currently, IDs are defined in the VAP as an unsigned byte array field of length 16. To allow applications to define the ID format (with the 16 byte constraint), all APIs that add a resource (rule, user, etc.) may optionally provide the ID to create the resource with. If not provided, the device will create an ID.

IDs within each type (Rule, User, View, etc.) should be unique at least on the channel level, but could be unique across devices. If the ID is not unique across devices, a globally unique ID could be derived by combining the device address and channel ID (or just the channel ID if it is unique). If the application-generated ID is not unique within its own type, a status code of 400 is returned when trying to add a new element with an existing ID. It is suggested that the channel ID be globally unique.

1.1.1.1.1 ID Encoding

While there is no inherent format to the ID except it being 16 bytes in length, there are restrictions on how it is encoded. Because IDs will occur as part of a URI, there are two ways to encode an ID: either following RFC 3986 or, for pure binary IDs, as a hex string.

RFC 3986 first converts the URI to UTF and then prints the following unreserved characters in the URI without any encoding:

- A-Z

- a-z

- 0-9

- -

- .

- _

- ~

All non-printable or reserved characters will be encoded as a two digit hex value prefixed by a %. For example, a space (ASCII value of 32) will be encoded as %20. This means the value of the ID is stored internally as 16 bytes, but the XML representation may be up to 48 characters in length if every byte is encoded.

Because a pure binary ID can contain values that might interfere with the operation of browsers and web servers, VAP supports hex encoding of the ID. The ID must begin with 0x (0X is also acceptable) followed by 16 pairs of hex values. Each hex pair represents a single byte in the ID. For example: 0x3F431245DE67FAC46F9D034CA23AEFD4. The hexadecimal characters A-F can also be represented by a-f. So 0x3f431245de67fac46f9d034ca23aefd4 is equivalent to the previous ID.

If readable IDs are desired, it is recommended that IDs are created with unreserved, printable ASCII characters. IDs less than 16 bytes in length will automatically be expanded to fill the entire buffer with nulls. However, VAP does allow removal of trailing nulls to improve readability on both the retrieval and insertion of IDs.

1.1)General Notes

- The starting point of all API calls is /api.rest. This is rooted at the starting point defined in the VAProtocol response.

- For floating point numbers, the values can have up to seven digits of precision.

- The format of timestamps is defined by RFC 3339. Times in VAP are always in Coordinated Universal Time (UTC). Examples of this format are:
  1999-01-09T13:30:50Z (January 9th, 1999 13:30:50 UTC)
  2002-03-01T05:05:33Z (March 1st, 2002 05:05:33 UTC)
  2007-04-07T11:15:13.444Z (April 7th, 2007 11:15:13.444 UTC)

- For timestamps, there will be up to millisecond precision.

- For lists of items, the naming scheme follows this format: XyzList contains XyzSummary items. XyzSummary has an XLINK attribute pointing to the real Xyz. List and Summary items cannot be modified directly, but are instead modified through their real underlying items.

- The XLINK href can be defined with any of the three common URI references: absolute (e.g. http://server/path/more/path), root relative (e.g. /path/more/path), or relative (e.g. path assuming the request was rooted at /path/more). The typical usage should be either root relative (as shown in this document) or absolute. Be aware that relative paths place more burden on the clients.

- In general, all resource names in URIs should be case-sensitive and match the case specified in this document. The only exceptions are the hex-encoded IDs explained earlier in this section.

- The location of images returned by the device can be rooted anywhere on the device. These image URIs do not have to be rooted under /api.rest.

1.2)Coordinate System

The coordinates used by VAP are normalized with their values ranging from 0.0000000 to 1.0 with 0,0 being the upper left corner. To calculate image coordinates from the normalized coordinates the following formula is used:

```
Image X = Normalized X * Image Width
Image Y = Normalized Y * Image Height
```

To calculate the normalized coordinates from the image coordinates, the reverse formula is used.

```
Normalized X = Image X / Image Width
Normalized Y = Image Y / Image Height
```

Objects that contain width and height are normalized as well. To convert the width and height values between normalized and image coordinates, the following formula is used:

```
// To rectangle width/height in image coordinates
Image Rect Width = Normalized Rect Width * Image Width
Image Rect Height = Normalized Rect Height * Image Height

// To rectangle width/height in normalized coordinates
Normalized Rect Width = Image Rect Width / Image Width
Normalized Rect Height = Image Rect Height / Image Height
```

To compute the lower-right image coordinates of the rectangle, the following formula is used:

```
// To rectangle width/height in image coordinates
Bottom X = (Normalized Rect Width + Normalized X) * Image Width
Bottom Y = (Normalized Rect Height + Normalized Y) * Image Height
```

2)*Conventions*

For brevity and formatting, the following conventions are used throughout the document.

- Text in a URI delimited by [ ] indicates a replacement value. The actual value depends on the resource being addressed, but it is typically an ID. If a URI contains **[channel root]**, the full URI would be /api.rest/channels/**[channel id]**.

- Properties are in **bold** text, and property values are *italicized*.

- ID properties are shortened to be easily readable in this document. For example, RuleID may be listed as "Rule009". The actual ID will differ.

Protocol Information

The protocol information describes the capabilities of the implementation of VAP on a device. Its purpose is to provide an application with the basic amount of information to ensure proper communication and support. An example of this XML is:

```
<?xml version="1.0" encoding="utf-8"?>
<VAProtocol xmlns:xsi="http://www.w3.org/2001/XMLSchema-instance"
        xmlns:xsd="http://www.w3.org/2001/XMLSchema"
        xmlns="http://www.objectvideo.com/schemas/ovready">
 <ProtocolVersion>1.1</ProtocolVersion>
 <Root>/some/location/prefix</Root>
 <SupportedDataFormats>
   <DataFormat>XML</DataFormat>
 </SupportedDataFormats>
 <SupportedAuthentications>
   <Authentication>HTTPBasic</Authentication>
   <Authentication>VAPSimple</Authentication>
 </SupportedAuthentications>
</OVReadyProtocol>
```

The **ProtocolVersion** property tells an application which version of VAP is being used. Much like HTTP, the intent is that newer versions are backwards compatible such that an application can default to the basic level of support. If a higher version is returned, an application can utilize it to provide better support for the device.

The **Root** property tells an application where all calls to VAP should be rooted. After the defined root path, all API calls start with /api.rest.

Device Configuration

One of the key components in the VAP design is the concept of a "device." A device physically hosts the video analytics software. Typically a device is represented by a single IP address. If a physical device has multiple IP addresses, each address is considered a separate device.

One device can handle multiple video "channels" of analytics. The configuration of a device affects all channels, but the configuration of a single channel does not affect the device.

The device configuration provides the details about the device as a whole. The device configuration is comprised of read-only and modifiable sections. The whole configuration is retrieved from the configuration root URI (/api.rest/device) but cannot be modified at this location. Each modifiable section has its own URI to retrieve and update that individual section.

Device Information

The **DeviceInformation** describes the device itself. This section is read-only.

The **ID** field is the unique identifier of the device itself. It follows the pattern for unique identifiers.

The **Manufacturer, ModelName,** and **ModelNumber** properties provide basic information on the device. If either **ModelName** or **ModelNumber** does not apply, it can be left blank.

The **FirmwareVersion** and **HardwareVersion** properties provide the version or revision numbers of the firmware and hardware, respectively.

The **AnalyticsVendor** property tells an application the source of the video analytics that is hosted on the device.

The **AnalyticsVersion** property tells an application which version of the analytics library is being used.

Operation	Method	URI	XML Data Type
Retrieve device information	GET	/api.rest/device/information	DeviceInformation

Supported Features

The **SupportedFeatures** section describes the features supported by this device. This section is read-only.

The **SupportsFirmwareUpdate** property tells an application whether the firmware can be updated. Currently VAP does not allow firmware to be updated through the specification, but the firmware can be updated through another mechanism. This property provides an application with the knowledge of which devices can (or cannot) be updated.

The **SupportsAnalyticsLicenseUpgrade** property tells an application whether or not the analytics license can be upgraded to new functionality through VAP. If the analytics license cannot be upgraded through VAP, upgrading the functionality can be done through another mechanism such as a firmware upgrade (if supported).

The **SupportsDeviceReset** and **SupportsChannelReset** properties tell the application whether the device can be reset as a whole or on a per-channel basis, respectively. If supported, the appropriate *Reset* operation can be performed on the device or a specific channel as detailed later.

The **SupportsAlertPolling** and **SupportsAlertStreaming** properties determine how the device will output alerts that are triggered. For those outputs that are supported, the appropriate settings must exist in the **AlertConfiguration** section for each channel. If either of these properties is *false*, any attempts to access the corresponding alert output mechanism either at the device or channel level will return a 403.

The **SupportedAlertPollingBufferSize** is the maximum number alerts that can be buffered on the whole device for **AlertPolling**.

The **SupportsCountTallyPolling** and **SupportsCountStreaming** properties are similar to the alert settings except they are specific to count output. If either of these properties is *false*, any attempts to access the corresponding count output mechanism at the device or channel level will return a 403.

The **SupportsSnapshots** property tells an application whether the device supports channel or view snapshots. If this property is *false*, a 403 will be returned when requesting a channel or view snapshot.

The **SupportedAnalyticsFrameSizes** property describes all supported resolutions for analytics. This will contain one or more supported resolutions.

The **SupportedSnapshotImageContentType** property describes the format of all images that are included in alerts or returned by the view and channel snapshots. The view and channel snapshots repeat this content type in the HTTP header. This type follows the standard HTTP content types (e.g. image/jpeg, image/x-png, image/gif).

The **SupportedContentTransferEncodings** lists the supported MIME encodings. All devices must support *x-identity*, but all the other types (*x-deflate*, *x-xml-token*, and *x-xml-token-deflate)* are optional.

The **SupportsSelectiveEventStreaming** property tells an application if the device supports specifying one or more channels to stream events using a single connection. If this property is false or does not exist, the device will stream all channels.

The **SupportedEventPushReceivers** property lists all the types of EventPushReceivers that this device supports. If this list is empty then the device does not support the event push mechanism. The event push mechanism is another alternative to deliver analytics events to an external application. Currently, the two valid types are **HTTPXMLEventPushReceiver** and **HTTPSXMLEventPushReceiver**. The former specifies that the device should push events as XML over HTTP. The latter is similar except it pushes events over HTTPS.

The **SupportsAuthenticationExtensions** property tells an application whether the device supports VAP authentication extensions to aid in login and logout.

Operation	Method	URI	XML Data Type
Retrieve supported features	GET	/api.rest/device/supportedfeatures	SupportedFeatures

Event Push Configuration

The **EventPushConfiguration** section describes the configuration of up to two **EventPushReceivers** working in either failover or redundancy mode. If the **SupportedEventPushReceivers** property in **SupportedFeatures** is empty, the **EventPushReceivers** section is also empty. Any attempts to modify the **EventPushConfiguration** in this case will result in an HTTP status code of 403 if the application does a PUT to the /api.rest/device/eventpushconfiguration URI.

The **EventPushConfiguration** section can be modified through the /api.rest/device/eventpushconfiguration URI. In addition, the **EventPushConfiguration** section can be individually retrieved from this same URI. The XML in both cases is:

```xml
<?xml version="1.0" encoding="utf-8"?>
<EventPushConfiguration
          xmlns:xsi="http://www.w3.org/2001/XMLSchema-instance"
          xmlns:xsd="http://www.w3.org/2001/XMLSchema"
          xmlns="http://www.objectvideo.com/schemas/TBD">
  <Mode>Failover</Mode>
  <EventPushReceivers>
   <EventPushReceiver xsi:type="HTTPXMLEventPushReceiver">
     <Address>192.168.2.122</Address>
     <Port>80</Port>
     <URI>/alerts/someform.asp</URI>
     <AuthenticationType>None</AuthenticationType>
     <User />
     <Password />
   </EventPushReceiver>
   <EventPushReceiver xsi:type="HTTPSXMLEventPushReceiver">
     <Address>webserver</Address>
     <Port>443</Port>
     <URI>/alerts/receive/someform.jsp</URI>
     <AuthenticationType>HTTPBasic</AuthenticationType>
     <User>fred</User>
     <Password>mysecretpassword</Password>
   </EventPushReceiver>
  </EventPushReceivers>
</EventPushConfiguration>
```

The **Mode** property determines how the device handles the **EventPushReceivers** if there is more than one defined. For a single defined receiver, this property is ignored. This value can either be **Failover** or **Redundancy**. **Failover** means that the device will only send to the second receiver if the first receiver failed. The order of **EventPushReceivers** determines the order of the failover. **Redundancy** means that the device will push to both receivers for every event. This may cause additional overhead on the device.

The **EventPushReceivers** property contains the list of the receivers. This can be an empty list if the device is not configured to push events. Each **EventPushReceiver** must be a valid type as defined in **SupportedEventPushReceivers**. The device must ensure that the order of this list is consistent whenever it is requested as it determines the failover order.

Each **EventPushReceiver** contains multiple properties. The exact properties are determined by the xsi:type. Currently, both the **HTTPXMLEventPushReceiver** and the **HTTPSXMLEventPushReceiver** contain the same properties. The **Address** property is the hostname or IP address of the HTTP server. The **Port** is the port of the HTTP server. The **URI** is location which the device will POST an event to. The **AuthenticationType** is the type of authentication that the HTTP server requires. This can be *None* or *HTTPBasic*. The **User** and **Password** properties define the credentials that are required to authenticate. These can be empty if they are not required.

Operation	Method	URI	XML Data Type
Retrieve event push configuration	GET	/api.rest/device/ eventpushconfiguration	EventPushConfiguration
Update event push configuration	PUT	/api.rest/device/ eventpushconfiguration	EventPushConfiguration

Channel Management

The channel configuration APIs need to provide a mechanism to get the list of all channels as well as information about specific channels. An example of the channel list XML is:

```xml
<?xml version="1.0" encoding="utf-8"?>
<ChannelList xmlns:xsi="http://www.w3.org/2001/XMLSchema-instance"
        xmlns:xsd="http://www.w3.org/2001/XMLSchema"
        xmlns:xlink="http://www.w3.org/1999/xlink"
        xmlns="http://www.objectvideo.com/schemas/TBD">
 <ChannelSummary xlink:type="simple"
          xlink:href="/api.rest/channels/0">
  <ID>0</ID>
  <Name>Parking Lot PTZ</Name>
  <AnalyticsType>OnBoard 1000</AnalyticsType>
  <IsAnalyticsEnabled>true</IsAnalyticsEnabled>
 </ChannelSummary>
 <ChannelSummary xlink:type="simple"
          xlink:href="/api.rest/channels/1">
  <ID>1</ID>
  <Name>Main Entrance</Name>
  <AnalyticsType>VendorType or Subtype</AnalyticsType>
  <IsAnalyticsEnabled>false</IsAnalyticsEnabled>
 </ChannelSummary>
</ChannelList>
```

The **ChannelList** returns minimal information about each channel to provide some context. However, it provides an XLINK attribute with a URI to follow to obtain more information about the channel.

The **ID** property is the identifier of this channel. It follows the ID conventions listed on page 80. This ID will be used to identify the channel in the **ViewInfo** on alerts and counts. It is also contained within the data provided by the metadata stream. If the channel identifier is not globally unique (or unique within an VAP deployment), the application may need to store additional information to uniquely identify the channel.

The **Name** property is an optional field that provides a user-friendly name for the channel if one is needed in an application. For example, an application could name the channel to reflect what it is analyzing.

The **AnalyticsType** property is the type of analytics that this channel is licensed for. This will contain either the name of the license key (e.g. *VendorType*) or a value of *None*. *None* indicates that no key is present and this channel is not licensed and therefore will not run.

The **IsAnalyticsEnabled** property specifies whether this channel is enabled for analytics or not. If the channel is not licensed, this value is always *false*.

Operation	Method	URI	XML Data Type
Retrieve list of channels	GET	/api.rest/channels	ChannelList

The **Channel** type adds to the properties defined by **ChannelSummary**. The XML for each channel is:

```xml
<?xml version="1.0" encoding="utf-8"?>
<Channel xmlns:xsi="http://www.w3.org/2001/XMLSchema-instance"
     xmlns:xsd="http://www.w3.org/2001/XMLSchema"
     xmlns="http://www.objectvideo.com/schemas/TBD">
 <ID>0</ID>
 <AnalyticsType>VendorType or Subtype</AnalyticsType>
 <Name>Parking Lot PTZ</Name>
 <VideoSource>video://0</VideoSource>
 <IsAnalyticsEnabled>true</IsAnalyticsEnabled>
 <IsAnalyticsCalibrationRequired>false
                    </IsAnalyticsCalibrationRequired>
 <IsAnalyticsCalibrated>false</IsAnalyticsCalibrated>
 <AnalyticsFrameSize>
  <Width>320</Width>
  <Height>240</Height>
 </AnalyticsFrameSize>
 <AlertConfiguration>
  <AlertPolling>
   <SnapshotOutput>true</SnapshotOutput>
   <TargetOutput>true</TargetOutput>
   <SnapshotsInline>false</SnapshotsInline>
  </AlertPolling>
  <AlertStreaming>
   <SnapshotOutput>true</SnapshotOutput>
   <TargetOutput>true</TargetOutput>
   <SnapshotsInline>true</SnapshotsInline>
  </AlertStreaming>
  <AlertPushing>
   <SnapshotOutput>true</SnapshotOutput>
   <TargetOutput>true</TargetOutput>
   <SnapshotsInline>true</SnapshotsInline>
  </AlertPushing>
 </AlertConfiguration>
</Channel>
```

The **ID** and **AnalyticsType** are read-only and any attempts to change these values will be ignored. The **ID** is determined by the device while the **AnalyticsType** is defined by the license key.

The **Name** property is the name of this channel that an application would display to the user.

The **VideoSource** property is an optional property that allows the application to configure what video source this channel is analyzing. For example, this could be a specific analog video input on the device, a sub-window of the video frame, or a reference to an IP video stream. Refer to the device documentation to determine if this field is required and, if so, what the acceptable values are.

The **IsAnalyticsEnabled** property specifies whether this channel is enabled for analytics or not. If this channel is licensed, the analytics can be enabled or disabled as necessary. If the channel is not licensed, this value is always *false* and any attempts to update this property will be ignored.

The **IsAnalyticsCalibrationRequired** property is read-only and specifies whether the analytics requires calibration. This depends on the analytics vendor and/or the license type. If this is *true*, this channel should be calibrated. This property does not indicate whether the channel has been calibrated or not. It only specifies that the channel may need calibration.

The **IsAnalyticsCalibrated** property is read-only and specifies whether the analytics has been calibrated or not. If the **IsAnalyticsCalibrationRequired** property is *false*, this property should always return *false*.

The **AnalyticsFrameSize** property lists the resolution currently being processed by the analytics. Changing this property will cause the analytics to restart to process the different resolution. If the given resolution is not supported, a 400 will be returned and the old value is retained. The supported resolutions are listed in the **DeviceConfiguration**.

The **AlertConfiguration** section describes how the alerts will be output from this channel. There is a section for each of the available output mechanisms: polling (**Alert Polling**), streaming (**AlertStreaming**), and pushing (**AlertPushing**). If alert output is not supported for this channel, then this section may be empty. If a particular output mechanism (e.g. polling) is not supported, then that configuration is not listed. The **SnapshotOutput** and **TargetOutput** properties specify whether snapshots and/or target information (basic information about the target such as a bounding box) is contained within the generated XML.

If **SnapshotOutput** is *false*, the **SnapshotInline** property is ignored and no markup will be output or snapshots be placed inside the XML.

If the **SnapshotsInline** property is *true*, a Base64-encoded snapshot will be placed in the XML directly instead of a URI pointing to the snapshot.

Operation	Method	URI	XML Data Type
Retrieve channel information	GET	/api.rest/channels/[channel id]	Channel
Update channel information	PUT	/api.rest/channels/[channel id]	Channel

Event Output

The VAP assumes the analytics platform outputs events in two forms: alerts and counts. The primary difference between these two output types is that alert output (for security applications) contains the full information about the alert including snapshots (if supported) and target (object) information, whereas the count output (for business intelligence applications) contains only the numerical value so as to reduce the bandwidth and storage requirements for count data. Depending on the rule and output mechanism, the numerical value for counts could be cumulative (e.g., the number of times a Tripwire was crossed) or instantaneous (e.g., the number of people in the area at this exact moment).

The three mechanisms to receive alert or count events are:

- on a request basis (polling) at both the channel and device level

- through an asynchronous mechanism where an application initiates the communication (streaming) at both the channel and device level

- through an asynchronous mechanism where the device connects and sends events to an external application (pushing) on the device level

Polling requires an application to request the alert or count information as needed and the frequency is determined by the application. Polling for alerts returns the list of all alerts in the device's buffer (the size of the buffer can be retrieved as part of the **DeviceConfiguration**) for the whole device or a specific channel. Depending on the frequency of polling, an application may receive duplicates from previous requests or may have missed some alerts altogether. Each alert has an ID to help the application reconcile alert lists.

Polling for counts does not return all the individual counts that are stored in the device buffer. Because of the nature of polling and the possibly limited buffer on a device, this approach may miss too many counts. Instead, polling returns a count tally for each rule. This tally is how many times the rule triggered since the tally was last reset.

Streaming of alert and count data pushes the information to an application as the events happen. Unlike polling, this mechanism is best suited for when the application needs every event as there is less likelihood of missed events as long as there is a listening client. Polling is useful for dashboard-like applications such as a web application hosted directly on the device, although it is not limited to such applications.

Pushing is similar to streaming except that the device is responsible for connecting to an external application (called an event receiver) and pushing the event. In streaming, if there is no listening application, the event is not passed along. VAP allows specification of up to two event receivers working in either a failover or redundancy mode. Pushing is best suited for networks where persistent connections are not feasible or reliable since the device can connect on demand to push the events. The push mechanism is only configured at the device level, although the individual channels can be configured to participate or not.

13. ANALYTICS ALERT SUMMARY AND RULE DEFINITION

Polling retrieves an Alert List, with each alert including the Alert Summary and Rule Info. Device can be polled for the full alert information. Streaming streams the full alert information in one package.

Analytics Alert

- Alert ID
- Timestamp
- Message (user defined)

Rule Info

- Rule ID
- Rule Name

Custom Response Fields

- Key/Value pairs

Event Synopsis

Type: Tripwire

- Direction (what actually occurred)
  - left to right
  - right to left
  - any direction
- Points (multiple)
  - X
  - Y

Type: Multi Tripwire

- Line Crossing Order
  - Before
  - Before or After
- Duration
  - Time
- Tripwires
  - Direction
    - left to right
    - right to left
    - any direction
  - Points (multiple)
    - X
    - Y

Type: Area of Interest Event

- Points (multiple)
  - X
  - Y
- Actions
  - Enter
  - Exit
  - Appear
  - Disappear
  - Inside
  - TakeAway
  - LeaveBehind
    - Duration
  - Loiter
    - Duration

Type: Camera Tamper

Type: Full Frame Event

- Actions
  - Enter
  - Exit
  - Appear
  - Disappear
  - TakeAway
  - LeaveBehind

Target Slices

- Time Offset
- Target ID
- BoundaryBox
  - X
  - Y
  - Width
  - Height
- Classification (actually classification output)
  - Anything
  - Human
  - Vehicle

Snapshot

- [string]

Analytic Count

- Count
  - 1 for triggered rule (just a tally) and dwell data rule
  - Occupancy value for occupancy rule
- Count Rule Type
  - Triggered Rule (event, such as tripwire)
  - Occupancy Data Rule
  - Dwell Data Rule
- Duration
  - 0 for triggered rule (just a tally) and occupancy rule
  - Dwell time in seconds for dwell data rule
- Timestamp

Rule Info

- Rule ID
- Rule Name